2nd Edition

Job-Hunting on the Internet

by Richard Nelson Bolles

author of What Color Is Your Parachute?

Job-Hunting
on the Internet

Job-Hunting
on the Internet

A DESKTOP COMPANION
TO THE WEBSITE

http://www.tenspeed.com/parachute

Second Edition
Revised and Updated

Richard Nelson Bolles

Ten Speed Press
Berkeley, California

Ten Speed Press
P.O. Box 7123
Berkeley, California 94707
www.tenspeed.com

Distributed in Australia by Simon and Schuster Australia, in Canada
by Ten Speed Press Canada, in New Zealand by Southern Publishers
Group, in South Africa by Real Books, in Southeast Asia by
Berkeley Books, and in the United Kingdom and Europe by Airlift
Books.

Library of Congress Cataloging-in-Publication Data on file with
the publisher.

Printed in the United States of America

3 4 5 6 7 8 9 10 - 03 02 01 00

Table of Contents

continued

continued

The Internet

Job-Hunting
on the
Internet

Acknowledgements

I want to begin by expressing my great debt of gratitude to those who gave me help in initially launching my Web site at washingtonpost.com: Jamie Hammond, Mary-Ellen Mort, Pete Weddle, Nick Donatiello, Margaret F. Dikel (formerly Margaret Riley), Martin Kimeldorf, Clara Horvath, Deborah Bryant, and my friend Guy Kawasaki.

Most of all, I want to express my gratitude for the immeasurable help I have received from my son, Gary Bolles, former editor-in-chief of *Network Computing* Magazine, and former editor-in-chief of *Inter@ctive Week* Magazine. He is one of the leaders in the field, and has been a fountainhead of knowledge and technical know-how for me.

Needless to say, none of the above are responsible for any of the opinions expressed in this book, or for any misstatement of facts which may be here, for which I alone am responsible.

My site is now located, of course, at
www.tenspeed.com/parachute

This Guide is a
desktop companion to the Website:

www.tenspeed.com/parachute

It is a copy of the Website as of Feb. 17, 1999 (with an additional Appendix), so that as you navigate the Website you may choose to read a particular passage either on the Website or in this Guide, as you find easier.

Equally, the Website is a companion to this Guide, with direct links already provided there for each of the sites described here in this Guide -- so that you do not have to laboriously type the URLs (the Web addresses) but can surf all the sites in this guide with ease by simply going to

http://www.tenspeed.com/parachute

Wherever you then want to visit, as described in this Guide, the site will take you there, with one mouse-click.

Note: The Website is updated regularly, so new information will be found there, that is not in this Guide.

Subjects

in This Introductory Section
Overview of This Guide
The Purpose of This Guide
The Structure of This Guide
The Guide's **Categories**
An Explanation of **My 'Parachute Picks'**
Gateway Sites
Gateways Maintained on Search Engine Sites

Sites

with Descriptions and Links
The Riley Guide   JobHunt
Job Pointer   InternetJob Surfer
The Argus Clearhouse: Employment
Career Resource Center

Employment Search Engines:

Yahoo   HotBot   100hot
Infoseek   Excite   Lycos   Magellan

1

An Overview of This Guide and Its Purpose

Thirty years ago, few had ever heard about fax machines, FedEx, cellular phones, desktop computers, e-mail -- or the Internet. But now, all these are omnipresent in our world. The revolution, in people's habits, is growing, and growing fast. Particularly with regard to the Internet.

Radio took 38 years to gain 50 million listeners. Television took 13 years to gain that number of viewers. The Internet, as we currently know it, took just 4 years to gain that number of users -- and now **over 72 million** Americans (35% of the U.S. population 16 years or older) are on the Internet, with 40 million more coming soon; the worldwide total of Internet users will be 327 million people by the year 2000.

The Internet's growth continues to be prodigious. The amount of information being processed over the Internet is doubling every 100 days, according to the U.S. Commerce Department. (4/15/98)

Some of that information is, of course, devoted to job-hunting -- and it is increasing along with all the rest. In 1995, there were just 500 job sites online; in 1998, an estimated 100,000 sites had some job listings or job information on them.[1]

---

1. Statistics from John Sumser, chief executive of IBN: InterBizNet, reported in Internet World, 4/13/98, p. 34. The article is online at
http://www.internetworld.com/print/1998/04/13/
intcareers/19980413-surges.html

Job-hunters' usage of the Web is also increasing. One measure of this: in 1994 there were 10,000 resumes posted online; in 1998, there were 1,200,000. I would guess that means that about 2,000,000 job-hunters are online during a typical month.

The numbers still represent only a fraction of the labor force. From an advertiser's point of view, two million is an impressive figure. In terms of a percentage of the total workforce, which now numbers 138,000,000, it's not. One survey firm confirmed that only 5.5% of the 99 million households in the U.S. had ever done any online job-hunting.[2] I would guess that means that about

2. These statistics are the latest available at this writing; they are courtesy of Nick Donatiello, President of Odyssey, a well-respected market research firm, and IntelliQuest, whose Feb. 5, 1998 Worldwide Internet/Online Tracking Service report is summarized on the Web at: http://www.intelliquest.com/ If you ever wish statistics about the Web usage, my favorite site (and recommendation) is Internet World's Cyber Atlas at http://cyberatlas.internet.com/

5,000,000 people are online during a typical year specifically to do job-hunting -- but really nobody knows. (Rating services' figures vary widely, and are therefore not to be leaned on with any confidence.)

All of this is certain to change, and people will start coming on the Internet in larger and larger numbers, over time, in order to job-hunt. But the question of the moment is: What's keeping them? Three reasons spring to mind.

(1) **Slowness,** of course. The Internet currently can be agonizingly s.......l......o.......w. That should change with cable modems coming, that are able to conduct operations at up to 100 times the current speeds. We will see. But there's also:

(2) **Bad word of mouth**. Currently, there are too many messages posted on the Internet and repeated in neighborhoods by disgruntled job-hunters, that run along the lines of "In spite of all the hype, Internet job-hunting is a total waste of time." Until that perception changes, job-hunters will still avoid the Internet in droves. Remember, if the survey (above) is correct, 94.5% of all U.S. households have not done any online job-hunting. Yet. And, finally:

(3) **Job-hunters need to know more exactly what goes on, on a job site.** Currently, the Internet is a world where reality and illusion are as seamlessly blended together, as they are in David Copperfield's show. In both cases, the audience can't figure out where reality ends and illusion begins.

Great harm can follow from this, in the case of the Internet. Job sites imply that to post a resume with them (and their search agent) is to ensure you will find a job -- but if your experience is that you don't find one, what you take out of that is lowered self-esteem. You think to yourself, *"What's wrong with me, that they're hiring everybody else, but not me?"* You are demoralized, and find it hard to continue your job-hunt with any enthusiasm. You are done in.

But, **you are being done in by an illusion.** In reality, a huge number of people who post their resume on the Internet don't find a job, thereby, If more people are to use the Internet for job-hunting, there needs to be more honesty about what is illusion and what is reality, on Internet job sites. That's the intent of this Net Guide.

I have visited every one of these sites myself, explored them (sometimes for hours) and decided how useful I think they are for the job-hunt task. Note: this guide is 50% experience (mine and others), and 50% opinion (all mine). Take it with a grain of salt. I just want you to know that my primary aim is to show you what is good (or bad) about the Internet for job-hunters, **so that your self esteem will not be 'done in' by the failure of the Internet to perform for you as advertised.**

My overall message in the Guide is this: if searching job listings (help wanted lists) on the Internet and posting your resume on the Internet doesn't get you a job, the problem is not with you. The problem is with the job-hunting system in this country: it's Neanderthal, on or off the Internet. (See diagram next page.)

OUR NEANDERTHAL JOB-HUNTING SYSTEM

6 "I will place an ad to find someone."

The way a typical job-hunter likes to hunt for a job (starts here)

5 "I will look at some resumes which come in, unsolicited."

4 "I want to hire someone for a lower level job, from a stack of potential candidates that some agency has screened for me."

This is called 'a private employment agency,' or -- if it is within the company -- 'the human resources department,' formerly the 'personnel department.' Incidentally, only 15% of all organizations have such an internal department.

3 "I want to hire someone for a higher level job, from among outstanding people who are presently working for another organization; and I will pay a recruiter to find this outstanding candidate for me."

The agency, thus hired by an employer, is called 'a search firm' or 'headhunter'; only employers can hire such agencies.

2 "I want to hire someone who walks in the door and can show me samples of their previous work."

"I want to hire someone whose work a trusted friend of mine has seen and recommends."

That friend may be: mate, best friend, colleague in the same field, or colleague in a different field.

1 *Employer's Thoughts:*

"I want to hire someone whose work I have seen." (Promotion from within of a full-time employee, or promotion from within of a part-time employee; hiring a former consultant for a regular position (formerly on a limited contract); hiring a temp for a regular position; hiring a volunteer for a regular position.)

The way a typical employer prefers to fill vacancies (starts here)

The Structure of This Guide

> "The Internet is merely an added dimension to the traditional job search, and it is not an easy dimension to add. Job-hunters need to focus less on the search for job listings and more on the idea of using the information accessible on the Internet as a tool for researching organizations and finding possibilities."
>
> Margaret F. Dikel,
> Author, *The Riley Guide*

The Categories

Generally speaking, I think it is not very useful to talk about "The Internet and job-hunting." It's too broad a subject, lumping too many things together, all at once.

It is more useful to break the subject down, according to the various tasks that a job-hunter may ask the Internet to do, as a part of their job-hunt.

There are essentially five such tasks. They are:

#1. As a place for you to search for vacancies listed by employers (often called want ads, job postings, or **job listings**).

#2. As a place to post your own **resume**.

#3. As a place to get some **career counseling** or job-hunting help.

#4. As a place to do **research** or find out information about fields, occupations, companies, cities, geographical areas, etc.

#5. As a place to make **contacts** with people, who can help you find information, or help you get in for an interview, at a particular place.

I have used these five headings (**Job Listings, Resumes, Career Counseling, Research,** and **Contacts**) as the structure for this Guide -- with an introductory section, **Gateway Sites**, that I will explain shortly.

My Parachute Picks --
My Personal Rating System

This guide is not intended to be a complete index of job-hunting sites on the Internet. There are alleged to be 100,000 such sites, with more being added, weekly. That's way too many to be useful to anyone.

So, I have tried to list only a few basic sites that I think are better than average in their category. You can call them **My Parachute Picks.** I try to explain, also, what's good about the site (the reality), and where you need to go with caution (the illusion).

From among all of my Parachute Picks, I have selected a few that I think are *especially* good, calling them "**My Parachute Picks +**," and giving them a Parachute symbol alongside their listing, thus:

= I think, for job-hunting purposes, this is one of the Best sites on the Net, *in its category*. As I just said, those categories are: **Gateway** Sites, **Job-Posting** Sites, **Resume** Sites, **Career Counseling** Sites, **Research** Sites, and **Contacts** Sites.

The views in this Guide are of course entirely my own, and not necessarily those of my Web publisher, tenspeed.com, or book publisher, Ten Speed Press. But I hope the six million readers of my book, *What Color Is Your Parachute?*, as well as other Web job-hunters, will find my opinions about Internet job-hunting helpful.

P.S. In spite of my spending as many as seven hours a day on the Internet, I'm just sure there are a lot of good sites that I know nothing about -- yet. If you as a job-hunter find a site that was particularly useful in your job-hunt, and you therefore think it should be listed here, please let me know; you can e-mail me at RNBolles@aol.com. Also, as Internet expert Mary-Ellen Mort says, Web addresses (URLs) turn bad faster than an egg salad, so if you click on a URL here and it doesn't work, please let us know immediately, at the same e-mail address. (We do the best we can on our own, registering our URLs with URL-minder -- http://www.netmind.com/url-minder/new/ -- and they send us e-mail when the URLs change; but, even so, we're bound to miss some.)

Parachute Picks: Gateway Sites

Gateway sites are simply explained: if you were to 'start from scratch' to find job-hunting sites on the Internet, you would go to your favorite search engine, type in such keywords as: "careers," "jobs," "employment," "resumes," "employers," "job listings," "job postings," "career counseling," etc., and see what it turned up. Needless to say, you would turn up something resembling a mudslide -- a huge mass of sites, in no particular order, badly needing sifting, organizing, evaluating and such, before the list was of any use to you.

But you don't need to face the mudslide. The job of searching, sifting, organizing, evaluating, has already been done for you by a number of people, and the results are posted on large "Gateway Sites" for the job-hunter or career changer. Think of them as "Carefully Organized Indexes of the Major Job Sites" with links.

Here are my favorites -- my **Parachute Picks** -- among those large indexes:

Gateway Sites

The Riley Guide

http://www.dbm.com/jobguide/

This is a justly-famous site on the Web. It's terrific, always has been, and since the beginning of 1998 is even more so, thanks to its creator, Margaret F. Dikel (formerly Margaret Riley). What you get here is a manageable index of the job-hunting resources on the Internet, well-organized, plus a lot of extras -- like: a wonderful summary of resume databases, and job-search guides. If I could only go to one gateway job-site on the Web, this would certainly be it.

http://www.dbm.com/jobguide/resumes.html
http://www.dbm.com/jobguide/jsguides.html

JobHunt: A Meta-list of Online Search Resources and Services

http://www.job-hunt.org/

This is another great site on the Web, with a fine summary of what's available to the job-hunter or career-changer. It's a large index of online job-hunting resources, well organized, and with evaluations (of sites' usefulness to the job-hunter). However, it hasn't been updated since July 1997, and isn't likely to be.

Job Pointer

http://www.dog-ear.com/

And now, to something truly different. The brainchild of Jeff Rios, it's a software file of bookmarks for job-hunters, together with a bookmark-manager program (DragNet Player 2.03), both of which you download through this site for free. Immediately you have, residing on your desktop, sitting outside of but operating within your favorite browser, 4,000 clickable bookmarks to job-hunting sites, organized in multi-level folders, by location of the jobs sought, or specific fields, or alternative work, or careers, or company & employer indices, or seasonal jobs, etc. You choose the folder accordingly, and then **Job Pointer** lets you click on URLs that whisk you within each site to the precise page and search-form for the kind of search you wanted, now displayed in your main browser window.

I think you could wander around in here for days. Good news: Job Pointer is updated every month or so, and once you download it you get monthly e-mail notification of updates, and how to download them. I think this whole bookmark approach is a great idea which can only get better -- as Jeff is continually improving it, often in major ways. *It is now available only for Windows users, I regret to report (there used to be a Mac version).*

Internet Job Surfer

```
http://www.rpi.edu/dept/cdc/jobsurfer/
```

Maintained by Rensselaer Polytechnic Institute, this site has an impressive list of job-hunting resources -- commercial organizations that have job databases, or resume listings, or other services -- all indexed alphabetically, with links.

The Argus Clearinghouse: Employment

```
http://www.clearinghouse.net/cgi-bin/
chadmin/viewcat /Business___Employment/
employment?kywd++
```

(That's three "underlines" between "Business" and "Employment" in the URL, in case you're ever typing this.)

This is another famous list, dealing with such topics as: careers, compensation, employment, jobs, labor, resumes, temporary employment, and workweek reduction.

Career Resource Center

`http://www.careers.org/index.html`

Here we go wide (as they say in the film industry). What do I mean? Well, when it's 3 a.m. and you can't sleep, you've tried all the obvious job-related stuff on the Net, and you're thinking "Is that all there is?" -- this is the place to come. CRC claims over 7,500 links to jobs, employers, newspapers, Internet Newsgroups, colleges, libraries, State Employment Offices, business, education and career service professionals on the Web, plus other career resources (including those in Australia, New Zealand, Japan, Germany, and United Kingdom as well).

Gateways Maintained on Search Engine Sites

Before closing this listing of my Parachute Picks for gateway sites, I should mention that some search engines or sites have their own index or "channel" of career and job-related sites on the Internet. These search engines function in fact almost as little career centers, with career help, advice, and so on. I have listed them below, in the order of my own personal preference -- beginning with my favorites, Yahoo and HotBot.

Yahoo! Employment

```
http://www.yahoo.com/Business/Employment/
```

HotBot

```
http:/www.looksmart.com/r?lm&ize&e71314
```

100hot

```
http://www.100hot.com/jobs/fullscreen.
html
```

It lists its idea of the 100 "hottest" sites dealing with jobs and careers.

Infoseek careers channel

```
http://www.infoseek.com/Careers?tid=421
```

Excite Careers & Education

```
http://www.excite.com/careers_and_
education/
```

Lycos Top 5% - - Careers

```
http://point.lycos.com/topics/Careers_
Overall.html
```

Magellan Internet Guide

```
http:/mckinley.com/magellan/Reviews/
Business/Jobs/index.magellan.html
```

Note: some of these search engines or search directories offer you their estimate of "the top sites," based on content and design. You as job-hunter of course want to know what are the top sites in terms of 'effectiveness at finding a job.' Unhappily, no one measures such an unimportant little detail!!!

This concludes my listing of the *gateway* job sites. Go look at them anytime that you want more suggestions than I offer in the five sections that follow. In the meantime, I suggest you choose whichever of these five sections in this Guide intrigues you the most, or read them in order one by one, viz:

#1. **Job listings** from employers.

#2. Posting your **resume**.

#3. **Career counseling**.

#4. **Research** on fields, occupations, companies, cities, etc.

#5. **Contacts.**

1.

Job Postings on the Internet

Subjects

17

Academic Jobs   **Government Jobs**
Legal Jobs   **Other Industries or Fields**
Temporary Jobs

Sites

in this section on Job Postings, with Descriptions and Links
Job Resources by U.S. Region
The World Wide Web Employment Office
The Monster Board (includes old Online Career Center)
JobSpace   Jobsite   Europages
Alta Vista Translation Service
America's Job Bank   CareerPath
JobBank USA   Internet Press
American Journalism Review
National Ad Search   CareerPost
HandiLinks to Agencies   Job Safari
CompaniesOnline   America's Job Bank
Employer's Direct   Whois Lookup
HeadHunter.NET   Weddle's Web Guide
JobBank USA: Jobs MetaSEARCH
Internet Sleuth   Career Search Launch Pad
Liszt   CareerMagazine   CareerMosaic
dejanews   Guide to Internet BBSs
Spam Hunters   Computer Virus Myths
JobTrak   Monster Board   JobSmart
The Black Collegian   Peterson's Summer Programs
Summer Jobs Location Search   Cool Works
Academia: The First Worldwide Register
Academe This Week   Jobs in Higher Education
The Federal Jobs Digest   FedJobs   FedWorld

continued

Sites, continued

<u>OPM's USA jobs</u>   <u>The Law Employment Center</u>
<u>Emplawyernet</u>   <u>Union College CDC</u>
<u>Job Listings by Industry</u>
<u>Job Databases by Professional Societies</u>
<u>APICS</u>   <u>Biospace.com</u>
<u>California Rural Healthcare Jobs</u>
<u>Communication Arts</u>   <u>Global Careers</u>
<u>Jobs in Mathematics</u>   <u>Kitchenette-Job Bar</u>   <u>NACUFS</u>
<u>Journalism Jobs</u>   <u>NASWCA</u>
<u>Net-Temps</u>   <u>Accounting/Finance Temporary</u>
<u>Information Technology Temporary</u>
<u>Administrative Temporary</u>
<u>Legal Professionals Temporary</u>

Out in the real world, they're called want-ads, or 'the classifieds,' job vacancies, or job opportunities. But on the Internet, they're called 'job listings,' or -- more commonly, now -- 'job postings'; sites where employers post the jobs they're trying to fill. These are the sites that make job-hunters just salivate, and are arguably the most popular job-related sites on the Internet.

But . . . the Internet is essentially selling a dream here, as though it were your fairy godmother. So before we get to the listings, let's briefly compare the dream with the reality:

The
Fairy Godmother Report:
Job Posting Sites

WHAT YOU'D HOPE TO FIND: A sure-fire way to find a job because you would have access to millions of vacancies, help-wanted ads, or 'job postings' listed on the Internet by employers, all at one central site, arranged by geographical area, searchable by a variety of criteria or keywords. An electronic fairy godmother, anxious to grant you your every wish.

WHAT YOU ACTUALLY GET: Las Vegas. 'Job-hunting slot machines' (which is how I prefer to think of 'job posting sites') that are bound to pay off eventually for someone -- often for a lot of 'someones,' but not necessarily *for you.*

You get: fragmented job listings online, not gathered together on one site, but spread out over hundreds if not thousands of sites, so that you don't know where to begin. You are offered no criteria for choosing the sites that are most likely to 'pay off' for you. You are only told which sites are the most active, in terms of either 'hits' or 'page views' or '(unique) visitors' -- but not which sites are the most effective -- where their visitors actually find a job. "We are one of the most visited sites on the

Internet" doesn't mean much. *It's not how many people come into a used car dealer's lot, that counts; it's how many go home with a car.*

You get: access online to only a fraction of the 16,000,000 employers that are out there, in the U.S. job market. Even the famous sites -- such as HeadHunter. NET, Monster Board, Career Mosaic, Career Path, America's Job Bank, and Career Builder -- each give you access, at best, to only .06% of all U.S. employers and 6% of all vacancies.

You get: access online to only a fraction of the 20,000 job titles that exist out there in the real world. I estimate that about 75% of online job listings are only for job titles in computer, engineering, electronic, technological, healthcare, financial, and academic fields. Vacancies in any decent number are not being posted online for the rest of the 20,000 job titles. Oh, people will keep telling you: "But the situation has improved greatly over the past two years." Yes indeed it has. But we've still got a *long* way to go!

You get: wonderful-looking 'shells' as I call the 'interfaces' or 'search forms' on the online job posting sites. They will list many different occupations, many different geographical areas. But I think of them as 'shells' because it's hard to know what's underneath them. When you go beneath those shells by clicking on non-technical job titles (like: "librarians") you will often find only one listing nationwide (or no listing nationwide) under that particular heading. Trust me: the vast majority of this nation's 20,000 job titles are still "missing in action" on the Net -- *beautiful looking 'shells' notwithstanding.*

You get: all in all, only a "sampling" on the Internet of the jobs available out in the real world. *Never take any site as a true picture of the job market!!!!!* It's skewed! (I'm being kind.)

HOW EFFECTIVE? My personal estimate of the effectiveness of Job Posting Sites on the Internet in helping you find a job: **two percent**, if the job you're looking for is not computer-related; **45 percent** if it is. That is to say, out of every 100 non-computer-jobs people who search job listings on the Internet, two of them may find a job as a result. I think 98 will not. And, out of every 100 computer people who search job listings on the Internet, 45 of them may find a job as a result. I think 55 will not. Consequently, my advice is: if you are job-hunting full-time, look to see what these job posting sites have. Who knows what you may find! But (big **but**) give no more than 3% of your job-hunting time each week to this particular online activity. Within that time frame, go to any site that looks interesting, and (metaphorically-speaking) pull the lever or push the button on that job-hunting slot-machine, cross your fingers, and pray you're one of the lucky ones. If you are, and it pays off for you, you'll think online job listings are the greatest invention since Swiss cheese; if not, you'll think the whole idea is full of holes.

WORDS YOU MAY HAVE CAUSE TO REMEMBER: You can search job listings on the Internet and find the perfect job you've always been dreaming of. But, you can also search all the job listings on the Internet and not find one single job that interests you. Don't take it personally, or think that this means there are no jobs out there for you. There are employers who want you -- keep that always in mind. They're just not on the Internet, or if they are: like little Bo Peep, they've lost some sleep, 'cause they don't know where to find you.

And now, to my favorites -- my Parachute Picks -- of the job listings sites:

Job Listings By Region: the U.S.

Job Resources by U.S. Region

http://www.wm.edu/csrv/career/stualum/
jregion.html

The true experts who guide actual job-hunters successfully in their search through job listings on the Internet are increasingly finding that the key to successful search is found on the regional sites more often than on the big national sites.

Focus, focus, focus -- they are discovering -- is the key. In the light of that, this is a key site on the Internet, with an absolutely wonderful list of local resources and job listing sites for each region in the U.S.

Job Listings By Region: the World

The World Wide Web Employment Office

http://www.harbornet.com/biz/office/
annex.html

This site has links to countries all around the world. Also, its employment opportunities are organized by occupation (over 700 occupational fields, in fact) rather than by industry. Outstanding!

Monster Board / O.C.C.

http://www.monster.com/

This site is that of the famous Monster Board. It has an index on the right: choose "International." This will bring you to over 1,000 global jobs. You can choose from about 50 countries around the world, or you can choose the Monster Board in Australia, Canada, the Netherlands, or the UK (United Kingdom).

Jobspace: Jobs Database

http://www.jobspace.com/

Also linking to countries outside the U.S., primarily in Europe -- and heavily weighted toward Belgium and Germany. What I like about this site is that it displays a list of the countries, with the number of jobs available in each. In other words (my favorite theme with job lists): you can tell what's underneath 'the shell' before you go beneath 'the shell.'

Jobsite

http://www.jobsite.co.uk/home/abroad.html

A United Kingdom site (as those who are experienced at reading URLs have already guessed), this has jobs in the U.K. (of course), Europe, and the Middle East. Not

24

necessarily a lot in every country -- as few as 13 vacancies listed, for some, when I visited.

Europages, The European Business Directory

http://www.europages.com/

For those looking for work in Europe, this site doesn't have a bulletin board or Web sites, but it does have 500,000 company addresses from over 25 European countries, with links to each country's Yellow Pages. You can search by country, subject, company name, etc. It also has a list (with links) to other sites that have economic data about Europe.

AltaVista Translation Service

http://babelfish.altavista.digital.
com/cgi-bin/translate?

If, in your search for jobs around the world, you encounter a page that is in a language you don't understand, copy down its URL, come then to this site, type in the URL, and babelfish (great name!) will display that troublesome page in English -- or in any other language you wish. (It's often only an 'approximation' of what the text says in its original language, but if you don't understand the original language at all, you'll appreciate having at least an approximation.) Hint: if you access this page more than once at one sitting, be sure and reload it. Otherwise your browser will just go to the 'cache' on your computer, and import the page with the listing stuck at the last URL you typed in. And I mean, stuck.

Job Listings from State Employment Service Offices

America's Job Bank

http://www.ajb.dni.us/

This site is maintained by the U.S. public Employment Service, and links 1,800 state Employment Service offices in the U.S. that -- as you might expect -- know about all kinds of job vacancies or postings: mainly full-time jobs, mainly professional, management, technical, clerical, sales, blue collar, etc. AJB lists between 250,000 and 750,000 vacancies daily, with 1,000 new listings added each day (but, as they themselves admirably point out, "this represents only a fraction of all jobs in the labor market.") Incidentally, if you ever see a job here that you're interested in, you then send your resume in as that employer directs -- often to the public Employment Service, for screening purposes. *Small problem: if your resume gets screened out, you won't necessarily be notified as to its fate.* (Ouch!)

Job Listings from Newspaper Classified Ads or Agencies

CareerPath.com

http://www.careerpath.com/

This site enables you to simultaneously search *some or all* of the current daily classified ads from almost 60 newspapers in the U.S. including *most* of the major ones (e.g., the *Washington Post, New York Times, Chicago Tribune,* and *Los Angeles Times* are included; but the *San Francisco Chronicle, USA Today,* and the *Wall Street Journal* are not). You can also search the ads from the previous two Sundays. The number of postings typically is over 230,000. I think this is a very useful site, *if* classified ads are what you are looking for, as it enables you to get at least a partial view of the job market in distant cities without having to move there or even subscribe to their local paper.

JobBank USA : Jobs MetaSEARCH

http://www.jobbankusa.com/news1.html

This meta-search site has a special section called Newspaper Search, and here you can link to the want ads of many U.S. newspapers that are not on Career-Path. You can only search through them one by one here, but they're handily grouped by state and area code. This list is thorough! In your geographical area of choice, you may find small newspapers (and therefore ads) that you didn't even know existed!

Internet Press: Newspaper Mania Job Center

http://gallery.uunet.be/internetpress/link40.htm

This is a *very* thorough site, with links to over 11,000 Internet News Sources.

American Journalism Review NewsLink

http://www.newslink.org/news.html

Here we go worldwide. At least 3,622 newspapers are now online worldwide, and they are all indexed (and linked to) here: national papers, dailies, business papers, campus newspapers, alternative papers, etc. Lots of papers, and of course, lots of classified ads. Very attractive and impressive site.

National Ad Search

www.nationaladsearch.com

Display ads in "help-wanted" sections of newspapers differ from normal want-ads in that they are more than one column in width, and tend to be for higher paying jobs. This site has about 10,000 of them, culled from the Sunday newspapers in over 60 metropolitan areas in the U.S., geared toward management, professional, technical and executive positions. Ads from the previous Sunday are displayed by Wednesday afternoon, usually -- some of them even go up on Tuesday. They stay for three weeks on this site. It is organized by the date the ad appeared, city, and job discipline: accounting, advertising, banking and finance, communications, computer/data processing, design and drafting, education, engineering, entry level, environmentalist-industrial hygienist, executive general, hospital-medical health, hospitality, human resources, insurance, legal, library, management, marketing, professional, purchasing, quality control, sales, scientific, technical, telecommunications, telemarketing.

There is a charge for using this site, $40 for six weeks, $75 for three months, but you can have a one week free subscription.

CareerPost

```
http://www.WashingtonPost.com/wp-adv/
classifieds/careerpost/front.htm
```

This site has job listings taken from the last two Sunday editions of the *Washington Post,* in a very clever display called JobView. It shows you in chart form, before you search, the number of ads they have online in various parts of the D.C. metropolitan area, sorted by occupational category. Terrific! The one downside is the date of the ad is missing until you click through to individual job announcements. Nonetheless, I wish every job posting site on the Web had a JobView display; it would let us see instantly what's beneath 'the shell' of some of those sites.

Incidentally, this site also links to CareerPath (see above), plus a few ads from the online *International Herald Tribune.*

HandiLinks To Agencies

```
http://www.ahandyguide.com/cat1/
employ.htm
```

We're talking links to employment agencies here, temporary agencies, talent agencies, modeling agencies, and every other kind of agent who is online and anxious to sign you up (often for a fee, of course) and try to place you.

Job Listing Commercial Sites on the World Wide Web

There are two kinds of commercial sites:

(1) **The first kind of commercial site on the Web is an individual employer's own Web site** -- often with 'help wanted' notices there.

Job Safari

http://www.jobsafari.com/

They claim this is the largest index of companies with employment information on the Internet, with fresh links to those pages -- categorized by alphabet and location. A nice place to start; still a lot of companies that I know are on the Web, and have employment information, are missing here. If there is a particular company or organization you'd like to work for, don't let lists be the last word: sometimes just typing the name of that company into your favorite search engine will turn up its Web site, and job listings thereon. Remember, the site isn't always named after the company. For example, Adams Media Corporation's job openings are on their CareerCity site.

CompaniesOnline

http://www.companiesOnline.com/

On this site you can search for information on over 100,000 Public & Private Companies. The site is co-sponsored by Dun & Bradstreet, and Lycos.

America's Job Bank

`http://www.ajb.dni.us/`

America's Job Bank has an impressive alphabetical list of (and links to) employers who have Web sites -- some 2,800 of them (of course you need to remember that's only .02% of the employers in the U.S.).

Employer's Direct

`http://www.rpi.edu/dept/cdc/employer/`

RPI (Rensselaer Polytechnic Institute) has a very good Career Development Center online, and at this site has put up a list of employers who place job opportunities on their own Web servers.

Whois Lookup

`http://alabanza.com/kabacoff/`
`Inter-Links/cgi/whois.cgi`

Here you can type in any part of an organization's name and it will look up to see what 'domain names' are registered to that organization (if any) on the Internet. (Try "Bumblebee.") It will tell you who to contact, and when the database was last updated on site. Created by Rob Kabacoff.

You can of course also use your favorite search engine to look for an employer's Web site. Suppose I wanted to work for some hotel on the shores of Lake Washington near Seattle. I go to my favorite search engine, which is Metacrawler, and type in the query: "Lake Washington hotel" and bingo: at the top of the list is the Web site of

"The Woodmark Hotel" and there is a section on that site called "Job Openings" (lucky me, were I a job-hunter: there were five openings when I looked).

You can also list any kind of employer, product, service, or business you're interested in, together with the words: "AND jobs." For example, your search query might be: "Publishing AND jobs."

(2) **Besides individual organizations, there's a second kind of commercial site, and that is a kind of employers' electronic bulletin board** if you will, where a number of employers come, to post their 'help wanted' ads, listings, vacancies, or postings -- use whatever word you will. Many of these are famous sites, and you will often see them discussed in the press, reviewed in magazines, and included on lists of job-related Web sites. Following is a list of the 'bulletin board' sites, beginning with my favorites - - my Parachute Picks:

HeadHunter.NET
http://www.HeadHunter.NET/

This is a commercial employment site belonging to Headhunters. LLC, and they give you access to the *original* job listings of 10,000 employers -- for the Web, a huge number. (But do remember that's still only .06% of the 16,000,000 employers in the U.S.)

One of the most popular job sites on the Web (along with CareerMosaic and Monster Board), they report 78,000 visitors a day -- some famous job sites only have 300 visitors a day. Last time I looked, HeadHunter.NET's postings came from 12,000 employers directly, and totalled 195,108 (none more than 45 days old). Unfortunately, 75% of them were only for high-tech jobs. That leaves 48,777 job listings here that are non-high-tech, and still you can "strike out." Going beneath its search form I found, *in some fields*, as few as four jobs posted, nationwide. The 'look' of this site has improved greatly!

Weddle's Web Guide

http://www.nbew.com/thisweek/index.htm

On the site of the *National Business Employment Weekly*, Peter Weddle has put up a fascinating Guide to the major job listing sites on the Web, giving us a great deal of information about each site. You will want to go there and see what he has to say about each job listing site. (Choose "Weddle's Web Guide" from the home page, and note that new stuff gets added regularly.)

His list has no links, but with the kind permission of the *NBEW* I have made up a chart, with links, of the sites he reports as having many job listings -- beginning with the highest number, and working our way on down. I have also listed the three fields that have the most listings on each site (taken again from Weddle's Web Guide). You will note immediately the predominant bias in site after site's listings: jobs in technology.

Some Commercial Sites With Many Job Listings Daily on the Web

Listed in descending order, most of these figures are from Weddle's Web Guide, using one typical period (January 1998) in order that the figures might be comparable. Note: I have not included in this chart a couple of sites that are on Weddle's list, viz., America's Job Bank or CareerPath, as they were listed here earlier, and I have added a couple of sites that are not currently on Weddle's list. The one thing you want to remember here is that these are the figures which the sites themselves reported to Weddle's Web Guide, and I think there is a great danger that some of these figures are inflated. But the Herculean task of independently checking the accuracy of these reports makes cleaning the Augean stables a snap, by comparison.

Number of Job Listings	The Three Fields With The Most Listings	Name of the Site and Its URL
153,000	Computer professional, engineer, accounting	**Headhunter.NET** www.headhunter.net
135,000	Computer science, engineering, management	**CareerCity** www.careercity.com
121,826	Executives, computers, sales	**GUARANTEED Job Search Success** www.joblynx.com

continued

Number of Job Listings	The Three Fields With The Most Listings	Name of the Site and Its URL
100,000	Computer science, engineering, management	**classifieds2000** www.classifieds2000.com
70,000	Engineering, mktg and sales, information technology	**CareerMosaic** www.careermosaic.com
50,000	Information systems, engineering, advertising/marketing	**The Monster Board** www.monster.com
45,000	Business/management, computer science, sales and marketing	**JobTrak** www.jobtrak.com
40,000	Technology, finance, management	**America's Employers** www.americasemployers.com
37,502	Information systems, engineering, marketing	**Net-Temps** www.net-temps.com
29,153	Programmer, engineer, manager	**Data Processing Independent Consultant's Exchange** www.dice.com

24,312	Engineering MIS, sales and marketing	**Westech Virtual Job Fair** `www.VJF.com`
20,000	Programming, engineering sales	**CareerMagazine** `www.careermag.com`
12,734	Information systems, management, engineering	**E.span** `www.espan.com`
12,691	Programmer/analyst, sales & mktg, engineering	**JobCenter Employment Services** `www.jobcenter.com`
12,163	Information systems, engineering, sales & marketing	**CareerWeb** `www.careerweb.com`
12,156	Executive, sales, technical	**careers.wsj.com** `www.careers.wsj.com`
11,000	Sales, computer engineering	**Best Jobs U.S.A.** `www.bestjobsusa.com`

**The Three Questions to Ask
About Job Listing Sites:**

If you visit these sites and find nothing that interests you, don't let your self-esteem plummet, or feel there's something wrong with *you!* Keep three questions (and answers) in the back of your mind as you visit these sites:

(1) **What makes some sites' figures so large?** Well, first of all, that site may be hugely popular with employers, and their figures may all be original postings the employers put up on that site. And/or: the site can copy postings from other sites such as newsgroups -- that's perfectly legitimate -- thus making their own site *look* hugely popular. And/or: the site can keep job listings up *forever*, (I've seen some currently listed with original posting dates of 10/96!). Sites should either tell you up front that there is a time limit on how long they keep a posting before automatically removing it -- say 7 days, or 30 days, or 45 days -- *or* better yet they should have a date stamp on each full ad or posting, as to when it was first put up!! If you see a job listing that looks interesting to you, be sure and see when it was put up. You want 'live' postings, not ones that have been 'dead' for two years.

(2) **What percentage of the total jobs available 'out there' do these postings represent?** Remember, there are 16 million U.S. employers 'out there' and they can create, in addition to jobs that fall vacant each month, two million new jobs in as brief a period as three months; on these sites, no matter how large, you are getting only a sampling of the jobs available 'out there.'

(3) **What's beneath the search form; is the site really wonderful, or does it only *look* wonderful?** You know what I mean: on the form are many different fields, many different occupational titles, many different geographical areas. But the problem with an online search form is that it is by nature a 'shell,' and only when you go beneath that 'shell' by clicking repeatedly on various categories and locations can you discover whether it's an empty shell or not. In many categories and locations on Web sites' search forms, you will draw a blank (no postings) time and time again, particularly when you look for non-technology jobs. Geographical "strike-outs" occur particularly often with the search forms of commercial sites that were originally regional, and are now *trying to look as though* they are national sites. But they aren't. At least yet.

The end of the matter is this: I would personally upgrade my own evaluation of these commercial sites from "okay" to "wonderful," if they each adopted the kind of online display chart (**JobView**) that the *Washington Post* has (see **CareerPost** above). If each site had that kind of a summary, you would know immediately what was beneath each 'shell.' But until they do, if you go beneath a particular site's 'shell' and find nothing in your specialty or region, console yourself with the fact that these sites offer you only a "sampling" of the job market. Which is fine, as long as you know that's what you're getting. Terrible, if you think these Web sites accurately summarize the total job market 'out there' -- as I have seen falsely claimed in the media.

Searching a Number of
Job Posting Sites on the Web
From One Site (Meta-Sites)

When you see a list of all the job posting sites above, the natural inclination is to think: "I don't want to have to go from site to site, to look at all these. I'd like to approach them all with one search engine, one entry, one click of the mouse." Well, unfortunately, you can't. But there are a few sites (often called Meta-sites or meta-search engines) that at least allow you to search up to 28 job posting sites -- all at once or successively -- from one page.

JobBank USA : Jobs MetaSEARCH

http://www.jobbankusa.com/search.html

I think this is the best of the metasearch job listings sites on the Web. It will help you search for vacancies on 28 of the most famous job listings sites or search engines on the Web, with but one entry, one query, one click of the mouse, on your part. Or, under National Search, you can search the famous sites just four at a time. An outstanding site!

Internet Sleuth

http://www.isleuth.com/empl.html

Internet Sleuth gives you, all on one page, the search forms for 13 job listings sites or search engines on the Web. True, you can only access the sites one at a time, by filling out its search form on this page, but the "Back button" on your browser will always return you to this page for the next try.

The Career Search Launch Pad

`http://www.pantos.org/cslp/`

The Career Search Launch Pad has the same basic layout, except it only gives you search forms for 5 job listings sites or search engines on the Web.

Job Posting Sites Elsewhere on the Internet: Newsgroups and Mailing Lists

The Internet is larger than just the World Wide Web. Outside the Web, lie USENET newsgroups, Mailing Lists, and a number of other modalities or protocols, as they are called. Many employers find these protocols -- especially newsgroups -- more effective than the Web, when they're searching for employees, most particularly when they're searching for technical employees. So it is to newsgroups you must go, and not just to the Web, if you're interested in those employers' job listings.

There are newsgroup metasearch sites (*on the Web, paradoxically*) that will allow you to search a number of these newsgroups or a number of Mailing Lists all at once, rather than having to go to each newsgroup one by one. Among these newsgroup metasearch sites, these are my Parachute Picks:

Liszt, The Mailing List Directory

`http://www.Liszt.com/`

Their technology "spider" goes out each week to search for all the major USENET newsgroups and all Mailing Lists anywhere in the world. Last I looked, it had 90,000 groups in its directory (and rising).

Using the keyword "jobs" with its Newsgroup Directory, turns up over 150 USENET newsgroups with job listings. Using the keyword "jobs" with its Mailing List Directory, turns up over 67 mailing lists, many of which feature job listings for particular occupations or handicaps, e.g., librarian jobs, software jobs, jobs for the blind, etc. You can find additional newsgroups or mailing lists by refining your search with keywords that specify particular job titles, industries, or geographical locations. Be forewarned, however, in spite of all these newsgroups' postings and this nice interface, you can still 'strike out.'

CareerMagazine

`http://www.careermag.com/careermag/`
`news/searchform.html`

Every day CareerMagazine downloads and indexes all the job listings "from all the major Internet jobs newsgroups," and then offers the ability to search these jobs by keyword, Location, Skills, and Title. You can designate "Most relevant jobs first," or "Most recent jobs first." Be forewarned, however, that in spite of all these newsgroups' postings and this nice interface, you can still 'strike out.'

CareerMosaic

```
http://www.careermosaic.com/cm/cm36.html
```

This site gathers over 60,000 job listings daily from over 80 USENET newsgroups. You can search them all at once, with specific parameters; their index is rebuilt every 24 hours "on a rolling basis;" and their postings are purged every seven days.

dejanews

```
http://www.dejanews.com/categories/
jobs.shtml
```

Has messages from over 80,000 Newsgroups, going back for two years. If it's job listings you're looking for, just type in your query, like: jobs AND Bay Area and it will give you the actual job listings that match, in reverse order (most recent, first).

Job Listings on Bulletin Boards

Besides the Internet, there are bulletin board services (called BBSs), which used to be accessed primarily if not exclusively outside the Internet. Now, most of them can be accessed through the Web; but a good list of them was compiled by a man named Richard Mark, featuring the Top 20 Internet BBSs for 1997; the list has not been updated since:

Richard Mark's "Guide to Internet BBSs"

```
http://www.cris.com/~rmark/sbi_idx/
sbi_new.htm
```

Job Listings by E-mail

Of course I'm talking about spam -- that wonderful avalanche of unwanted job offers that you receive daily in your e-mail box (if you're unlucky) notifying you of incredible jobs where you can work at home for a few hours a week, and still make $250,000! Or order just five reports and then sell them to everyone you hate. They're always written, of course, by people who are former customers.

No matter how badly your job-hunt is going, no matter how good these offers are starting to sound -- they ooze *sincerity* -- the two warning bells you want to always listen for, are: did they mention money (yours), and did they mention a check or credit card (yours)? If so, you know how they're putting bread on their table, clothes on their back, and a roof over their heads -- but there's absolutely no guarantee you will too. If you're *ever* tempted to hand them even a little of your money, for the huge rewards they *promise* will follow -- lie down; it will pass. Go to Las Vegas if the temptation persists; the odds there are better. My advice? Hit that Delete button or just ignore these 'job offers.'

Spam Hunters

```
http://www.zdnet.com/zdnn/content/
zdnn/0906/zdnn0001.html
```

If you've got loads of time on your hands, you might want to go further and *try* to reduce the volume of spam in your e-mail box. (Lotsa luck!) The site that offers you some suggestions (and links) to that end, is Spam Hunters.

Computer Virus Myths

http://www.kumite.com/myths

And while you're at it, you might want to brush up on 'hoaxes', designed to ensnare the innocent (the kind of e-mail that is always betrayed by this telltale phrase: "Tell all your friends!") For help in combatting *that*, a helpful site is Computer Virus Myths.

Focussed Job Listings

"The more focussed the job posting site, the better," says Internet job-hunting expert, Mary-Ellen Mort. "It should be focussed by geography, industry or occupation." (In this search for a focussed site, don't forget associations and journals. No matter how narrow your job specialty is, there's likely to be an association or journal or Web site with job listings. To find it, use your favorite search engine, type in your job specialty, and see what it turns up.)

JobSmart -- Upcoming Career Fairs

http://jobsmart.org/resource/fairs/
jobfairs.htm

Still another career fair/job fair site.

The Black Collegian Online

http://www.black-collegian.com/
jobs/jobsearch.html

The premiere career site for students and professionals of color, it has improved a great deal over the past couple of years. But the fact that it still has job listings with sentences like: "Respond before Nov. 15, 1997" five months later than that, tells me they've still got work to do.

Peterson's Summer Programs for Kids/Teens

http://www.petersons.com/summerop/
ssector.html

A great list, sorted alphabetically, geographically, and many other ways.

Summer Jobs Location Search

http://www.summerjobs.com/do/where

Lists a sample of summer jobs around the world: by "sample" I mean, when I visited the site in the Spring of 1998 it had 550 Summer jobs listed for the U.S., but only one each for Austria, Colombia, Germany, Holland, India, Norway, China, Russia, South Africa, Scotland, South Korea, Sweden, and Thailand. On the plus side, it had a nice summary page right up front, that was very candid about all of this.

Cool Works

`http://www.coolworks.com/showme/`

Links to more than 35,000 leisure jobs in National Parks, Resorts, Cruises, Camps, Ski resorts, Jobs for RVers, Ranch jobs, plus Volunteering, are to be found here.

Academic Jobs

Academia: The First Worldwide Register

`http://psy.anu.edu.au/academia/`

Maintained by Australian National University in Canberra, Australia, this site gives you a worldwide listing of academic positions vacant in teaching and research establishments, organized by subject and location. Institutions and organizations can post their positions for free. Thirty disciplines or fields are featured, plus interdisciplinary positions. Very impressive. Other academic sites:

Academe This Week -- Job Openings

`http://chronicle.merit.edu/.ads/.`
`links.html`

The job openings from the current issue of the *Chronicle of Higher Education*. Last I looked it was running around 900+ ads per week.

Jobs in Higher Education

```
http://www.gslis.utexas.edu/~acadres/
jobs/index.html
```

This is another good source of job listings in academia. Links to over 1,300 colleges.

Government Jobs

Government Jobs are to be found at a number of sites, including the following four:

The Federal Jobs Digest

```
http://www.jobsfed.com/
```

Under the heading, "Live Jobs," they list over 3,700 Federal vacancies on a typical day. Has a nice interface -- the jobs are sorted by occupation groups -- and displays several listings at the same time, in detail.

FedJobs . . . Federal Job Search on the Web

```
http://www.fedjobs.com/bestjob.htm
```

They list over 8,000 vacancies on a typical day, including non-federal job opportunities; and they have a fine search form. You can have a free preview of their listings, using that search form; after the preview, you have to be a subscriber to access further job listings on this site (subscription begins at $19.97 per month for unlimited use). I like their interface, plus they seem to list lots of jobs. This site has vastly improved over the past year or so.

FedWorld Federal Jobs Search

```
http://www.fedworld.gov/jobs/
jobsearch.html
```

This is an official U.S. government site, and is a gateway to more than 100 government bulletin boards. Not surprisingly, its postings are similar to those found in The Federal Jobs Digest (above), but you have to click on each listing one by one, in order to see each in detail.

OPM's USAjobs

```
http://www.usajobs.opm.gov/
```

This is another of the U.S. Government's official sites for jobs and employment information. It is absolutely current, but its search form hides what's underneath; when I went noseying around there, it seemed to me it had a slim selection in a number of job categories.

Legal Jobs
The Law Employment Center

```
http://www.lawjobs.com/
```

This site is sponsored by the *Law Journal,* and lists not only hundreds of permanent positions but also temp positions, employment trends, the nation's largest law firms, the *U.S. News and World Report* 1998 rankings of law schools, and other useful info for the job seeker.

EmplawyerNet

```
http://www.emplawyernet.com/
```

Emplawyernet.com has now formed an alliance with Lexis-Nexis, which should bring many improvements to the site. You can access it, without charge, for ten days, or -- if you're a law student -- for three months. Then it costs ($9.95 a month, but there are discounts for various groups).

Industries or Fields

Union College Career Development Center

```
http://www.union.edu/career/CDC/
CRH.LIB.WWW.html#APR
```

Union College has a very good list of Web sites for liberal arts graduates, Web sites organized by career field, Web sites for those desiring to work overseas, etc. An impressive list.

Job Listings by Industry

```
http://www.eresumes.com/links_jobs.html#
```

A good list of job listing sites for particular industries and occupations (Nannies, Hospitality, Broadcasting, Advertising, etc.)

Job Databases by Professional Societies/ Other Institutions

```
http://www.rpi.edu/dept/cdc/society/
```

It's a rather select list, but it's alphabetized by the name of the Professional Society, so it's easy to look at and worth giving a try.

Other sites for particular fields:

American Production and Inventory Control Society

```
http://www.apics-west.org/jobsum.cgi
```

Biospace.com

```
http://www.biospace.com/b2/
jobs_region.cfm
```

California Rural Healthcare Jobs

```
http://www.ruraljob.cahwnet.gov/
ruraljob/QUERY4.HTM
```

Communication Arts: Business and Career

```
http://www.commarts.com/bin/ca/bc_jl_o
```

Global Careers

```
http://www.globalcareers.com
```
For those in the fields of commerce or transportation.

Jobs in Mathematics

```
http://www.phds.org/
```
For those who love mathematics, science and engineering.

Kitchenette - Job Bar

```
http://www.kitchenette.com/jobs/
index.html
```

National Association of College & University Food Services

http://www.nacufs.org/

Journalism Jobs

http://ajr.newslink.org/newjoblink.html

The world's largest listing of jobs in journalism.

National Association of Social Workers

http://www.naswca.org/jobbulletin.html

Temporary Jobs

Net-Temps

http://www.net-temps.com

Here staffing agencies come when they're looking for temp workers -- 1,000 such agencies, in fact. Here also employers can come. Here also you as job seeker can come, to search by State or City, job functions or skills.

Accounting/Finance Assignments

http://www.metacrawler.com/marketplace/careercenter/

For Information Technology Consultants

http://www.metacrawler.com/marketplace/careercenter/

In the Administrative Field

```
http://www.metacrawler.com/marketplace/
careercenter/
```

For Legal, Financial, and Information Jobs

```
http://www.metacrawler.com/marketplace/
careercenter/
```

If you try job posting sites,
and they turn up nothing that interests you,
see page 175, or click here for:
"If You Strike Out, and Can't Find A Job"

2.

Resume Sites on the Internet

Subjects

in This Section on Resume Sites

Success Rate of Resumes

The Fairy Godmother Report on Resume Sites

What You'd Hope to Find   What You Actually Get

How Effective   Words to Remember

Building A Resume (Electronic or Otherwise)

Making Your Resume Look Better

For the Tongue-Tied (and Right Brained People)

Portfolio Resumes

Major Sites Where You Can Post Your Resume

Chart   **Other Resume Sites**

Sites Where You Can Hide Your Identity

"Search While You Dream" Programs

53

Sites

in this section on Resume Sites,
with Descriptions and Links

The Best Online Articles   JobSmart

Damn Good Resumes   ProvenResumes

Resumix   Rebecca Smith's Site

Resumail   200 Letters for Job-Hunters

Artists Portfolios   Your Portfolio Resume

Portfolio Library   Resume Services

Weddle's Web Guide   America's Talent Bank

HeadHunter.NET

World Wide Web Employment Office

The Riley Guide's List   JobBankUSA's List

bridgePath   ResumeBlaster

Many job-hunters think this should be the second best use of the Internet for their job-hunt: a place to post their resume. Oh my! Let's recall some simple truths, here: *a resume is a resume is a resume.* As readers of *What Color Is Your Parachute?* know, it's usually not a very effective job-hunting tool; normally, for every 1,470 resumes sent floating around 'out there' by various job-hunters, only one job-offer is made and accepted.

I'd like to be able to report that putting your resume online changes all that for the better; but the Internet is essentially selling a dream at this point. Time to compare the dream with the reality, in our second Fairy Godmother Report:

The
Fairy Godmother Report:
Resume Sites

WHAT YOU'D HOPE TO FIND: You'd hope that the Internet would turn out to be your Resume Fairy Godmother: that on the Internet there would be one central place to post your resume, and that to this one site all employers would come, whenever they wanted to fill a vacancy. There, using keywords, geographical location, and job title, said employer could quickly find a matching resume: yours. Voila! You'd be hired. The two-hour job-hunt.

WHAT YOU ACTUALLY GET: While it is obvious that online resumes do sometimes lead to a job, it is also obvious that in a large number of cases -- I'd even say depressingly-large -- *nothing* happens. Zero. Zip. Nada. Your beautiful resume is just sitting there on the Internet. And sitting there. And sitting there. And sitting there.

Want proof? You'll see it when you come to <u>The Chart</u> on page 65. Some of the results you'll see there: one famous resume site had 59,283 resumes posted on it, but only 1,366 employers looked at any of those 59,283 during the 90 days previous to the survey; another site had

85,000 resumes, but only 850 employers looked at them; another had 40,000 resumes, but only 400 employers looked at them; another had 26,644 resumes, but only 41 employers looked at them, in the 90 days previous. If you don't find these statistics depressing, I certainly do -- and would, even if you multiplied the number of employers by 100, in each case.

What's the problem here? Why doesn't your resume get more attention, *online?* Well, for a resume to achieve results online, some employer:

• **has got to be** *desperate* to find someone like you; and

• has got to be at the point, in their search for someone like you, that **they are reduced to reading resumes** (many employers' least favorite way of filling a position; they'll try anything else, first, since they regard the task of reading resumes as just this side of having a root canal); and then this employer

• **has got to go online** looking for a resume posting site (and remember, there are *at least* 10 million U.S. employers -- not to mention other countries' -- who don't even *think* of the Internet when it's time to hire); but if they do, then this employer

• **has got to accidentally stumble across the site** where you posted your resume -- and there are hundreds of such sites on the Internet; and then this employer

• **has got to accidentally stumble across your resume on that site**; and then this employer

• **has got to take the time and trouble to read it**, and then this employer

• **has got to take the time and trouble to print it out**, in all its blah ASCII sameness; and then this employer

• **has got to decide, after studying it, that they like it enough to invite you in**. (Note that the survey above only said "*looked at*," it didn't say "*chose*." Many employers *look at* resumes without finding any that they are interested in. Ho boy!)

Amazingly, with all this, you can still run into job-hunters (particularly if they're 'tech-oriented') who will tell you they found a job by posting their resume on the Internet. And they're very vocal about it. Of course, there are the thousands and thousands of job-hunters who posted their resume and never got so much as a nibble. They're very silent about it. Trust the silent majority!

Hold on tight to this simple truth: the Internet is selling a dream here, or an illusion: the illusion that you are doing something about your job-hunt by posting your resume online -- when in a huge majority of cases nothing is happening. And I mean: *Nothing.*

HOW EFFECTIVE? My personal estimate of the effectiveness of Resume sites on the Internet, in light of the above: **less than one half of one percent**, if the job you're seeking is not computer-related; **20 percent** if it is. That is: out of every 100 computer people who post their resume on the Internet, 20 of them will find a job as a result. I think 80 will not. And out of every 100 non-computer people who post their resume on the Internet, less than 1 of them will find a job as a result. 99 will not.

WORDS YOU MAY HAVE CAUSE TO REMEMBER: Sure, if I were job-hunting tomorrow I'd post my resume online. But I'd be very realistic about the likelihood that this will produce no result whatsoever. And once I'd posted my resume, I'd not wait another minute to go out and 'pound those pavements!'

If posting your resume online causes you to stay at home and wait for 'something' to happen, then (as job expert Mary-Ellen Mort says) these resume sites have become 'a flytrap for the lazy.'

Building A Resume
(Electronic or Otherwise)

A resume posted on the Internet is called 'an electronic resume.' When you want to know *how* to create one, you'll discover there's no shortage of advice online. Sites will tell you *how* to do it, and *where* to do it. They'll tell you the rules about scanning, and the rules about keywords, and so forth. Lots of advice. The question is: is it good advice? Well, sometimes yes, sometimes no. I don't think there's any subject job experts disagree more on than resumes. Anyway, from among all the resume advice sites, here are my Parachute Picks -- the ones I think are most helpful:

The Best Online Articles
about Writing A Resume

```
http://www.golden.net/~archeus/
reswri.htm#Articles2
```

Canadian author and job expert Gary Will has done a marvelous job, not only of listing (and linking to)

dozens of articles on the Web about resume writing; *but* of writing cogent and tremendously insightful reviews of each of those articles. He is very expert! Truly, an outstanding site! (Be sure and scroll down from the top of his page, as the reviews start the third screen down.)

JobSmart

```
http://jobsmart.org/tools/resume/
index.htm
```

If I were interested in putting an electronic resume on the Internet, and if I could visit only one U.S. resume site for guidance and help, JobSmart would surely be it. This site, the creation of a genius named Mary-Ellen Mort, features the best online summary about electronic resumes you can find, written by Yana Parker and Clara Horvath.

Yana is the author of the popular *Damn Good Resume Guide* series, and in addition to her helpful advice here, has her own Web site, **Damn Good Resumes**, while Clara teaches expert classes in this subject. JobSmart has a number of links to other resume sites on the Web, plus a *sample* list of places on the Internet where you can post your resume, free or for-fee.

```
http://www.damngood.com/jobseekers/
tips.html60
```

Proven Resumes

```
http://www.provenresumes.com/reswkshps/
electronic/electrespg1.html
```

On this site called ProvenResumes.com, maintained by Regina Pontow, some very helpful directions about constructing an electronic resume are contained in an article called "Scannable Resumes." Other topics include: "Hard Copy versus Electronic Resumes," "Biggest Mistake of Electronic Resumes," etc. In addition to these online articles, she also sells pamphlets (you can immediately download from her Electronic Bookstore) and books, on related topics.

Resumix

```
http://www.tripod.com/explore/
jobs_career/resume/
```

If you want to actually build your resume online, there's a site that will lead you step-by-step through the compiling of a 'plain vanilla' resume, and then format it for you, and submit it. The site is maintained by Tripod. Registration required.

Rebecca Smith's eRésumés & Resources

```
http://www.eresumes.com/tut_posting.html
```

When you've got your electronic resume all done, and you wonder where you should post it, this site has some good guidelines, and specific instructions about how to post on some of the better known sites (9 currently).

Note: This site also has good resume writing tips, and interesting examples of Web resumes.

Making Your Resume
Look Better

If you mail your resume, you can make it look as nice as you wish; but if you have to send it by e-mail, as is often the case, it's going to look *very bland* in plain old ASCII e-mail font -- stripped of all its lovely formatting and the 'nice look' of the original. There are three things you can do to counteract this:

(1) Put a sentence at the end of your resume such as the one that career expert Martin Kimeldorf suggests: "An attractive and fully formatted hard copy version of this document is available upon request." OR

(2) Using AOL 4.0, or Netscape Communicator's "Messenger," or Microsoft Internet Explorer 4's "Outlook Express," or Eudora Light 3, or a Windows software browser plug-in called "Resumail," (http://www.resumail.com/) you can format your resume. There are conditions in some cases: with AOL, for example, the employer or hiring authority must be on the AOL network; with Resumail, the employer must be on the "Resumail Network," and use Windows (95/98 or 3.x). OR

(3) Messenger and Outlook Express allow you to send your resume as an HTML file, with any or all of the features of the Web, including clickable Web addresses -- all this assuming your target employer knows how to read it!

For the Tongue-Tied
(and Right Brained People)

<u>200 Letters for Job-Hunters</u>

http://www.careerlab.com/letters/

Turning from resumes to letters, here's the best collection of them on the Internet -- 239 of them in fact. Author William S. Frank has put his entire book, *200 Letters for Job-Hunters,* online for free. (*Bravo! Bravissimo!*) So now, if you want to write something during your job-hunt, but just don't know how to write it, come to this site. There are cover letters galore, cold-call letters, thank-you letters (19 of them), also letters on how to leave a job gracefully, or how to negotiate a pay raise, etc., etc.

Portfolios

An alternative to the written resume is a pictorial resume, often called "a portfolio." It's not just *pictorial;* it intends to offer proof that you have the skills you claim to have. Certain professions are known for using a portfolio (artists, etc.) See:

<u>Artists' Portfolios</u>

http://www.rit.edu/~964www/Student/
JobSearchInfo/portfolio_sample_work.htm

But in the '80s and '90s, under the influence of books by career experts Eugene Williams, Martin Kimeldorf and others, the idea has been expanded to include many other professions.

For an introduction to the subject, see:

Your Portfolio Resume

http://www.talent-net.com/

On this 'fee site' called 'Talent-Net' (I am not recommending you buy their services) they have a free, good though brief introduction to the subject of portfolio resumes as they can be used by other professions besides artists. (Choose: "Promoting Your Qualifications with a Portfolio.")

For greater detail, go to:

Portfolio Library

http://amby.com/kimeldorf

Here Martin Kimeldorf describes in great detail his view of what a portfolio can be -- the why, the wherefore, and the how to. His form is not by any means the only way to go -- it's long, and directed at educational situations -- but it may stimulate your own creativity. His sample portfolio is at:

http://www.careermag.com/portfoli.pdf

Resume Services

http://www.yahoo.com/Business_and_Economy/
Companies/Employment/Resume_Services/

Reduced to tears at the thought of having to write your own cover letter and resume (electronic or otherwise), even with all these aids online? Here is a long list of agencies and individuals who will rescue you (for a fee of course). It's a long list.

How do you evaluate who's good and who's not, on this list? Answer: ask to see samples, first, "of resumes *that actually resulted in a job* for your client." Ask to talk afterward to the client to confirm that this was so. (Some resume writers will balk at this request; the good ones won't.)

Major Sites Where You Can Post Your Resume

Do remember that posting your resume online is the equivalent of nailing your resume to a tree in the town square -- where every employer, solid citizen, salesperson, con-artist, pervert, and drunk can see it, and copy down whatever he (or she) wants from it, for follow-up. *Think about it!*

Job expert Gary Morris suggests that if you are posting your portfolio or resume to a public area (such as a Web site) or an online resume database, security should always be a consideration. Gary advises job-hunters to "never include personal or contact information in the body of your resume for safety and security purposes."

I would say that you may want to give your e-mail address and your phone number (*'cause this is most employers' favorite way of contacting job-hunters*), but **not** your street address, nor business address, nor names of past employers or references *online.* You can always mail this information to an interested employer or recruiter *after* they have contacted you by phone or e-mail.

Anyway, here are some of the better known resume sites, starting with a summary of same.

Weddle's Web Guide

`http://www.nbew.com/`

On the site of the *National Business Employment Weekly,* Peter Weddle has put up a fascinating Guide to some of the major resume posting sites on the Web, giving us a great deal of information about each site. (New stuff gets added regularly.) You will want to go there and see what he has to say about each site in detail.

There are no links from his Guide to the sites, but with the permission of the *NBEW,* I have made up a chart with links, of the sites he reports as having the most resumes posted. Be sure to read the Note, immediately below, *before* consulting the chart.

U.S. Commercial Sites With Many Resumes Listed on the Web Daily

(Note: Down through this century, it has always been true: *job-hunters* flock to a new technology or job-hunting aid, but comparatively few *employers* do. As I mentioned earlier, if you look at this chart, you will see this clearly. One site has 59,283 resumes, but only 1,366 employers looked at them during the 90 days previous to this survey; another has 85,000 resumes, but only 850 employers looked at them; another has 40,000 resumes, but only 400 employers looked at them; another has 26,644 resumes, but only 41 employers looked at them. Unlike job posting sites, where the more listings there are, the better your chances, with resumes what you want is a famous site with the fewest resumes for the employers to choose from -- so there aren't 3,000 resumes just as good as yours competing for attention from this one employer.)

Number of Resumes Here	Charge for Posting Your Resume?	Employers Searching Here in Last 90 Days	Name of the Site and Its URL
275,000	No	(Figure not available) Only 25,000 Job Listings	**The Monster Board** www.monster.com
200,000+	No	(Figure not available) Only 10,000 Job Listings	**NationJob Network** www.nationjob.com
150,000	No	(Figure not available)) Only 45,000 Job Listings	**JobTrak** www.jobtrak.com
125,000	No	(Figure not available) Only 4,034 Job Listings	**CareerSite** www.careersite.com
120,989 Technical jobs	No	(Figure not available) 100,000 Job Listings	**PassportAccess** www.passportaccess.com
85,000	No	**850** employers 37,502 Job Listings	**Net-Temps** www.net-temps.com
70,000	No	(Figure not available) Only 3,500 Job Listings	**Career.Com** www.career.com
59,283	No	**1,366** employers 24,312 Job Listings	**Westech Virtual Job Fair** www.VJF.com

continued

GUARANTEED **Job Search Success** www.joblynx.com	(Figure not available) 121,826 Job Listings	Yes	56,945
CareerMosaic www.careermosaic.com	(Figure not available) 70,000+ Job Listings	No	55,000
Town Online Working www.townonline. com/working	**400** employers Only 1,000 Job Listings	No	40,000
E.span www.espan.com	(Figure not available) 12,734 Job Listings	No	38,000
HotJobs www.hotjobs.com	(Figure not available) Only 3,627 Job Listings	No	30,723
US RESUME www.usresume.com	**15** employers (new) Only 350 Job Listings	No	30,000
America's Employers www.americasemployers.com	**41** employers 40,000 Job Listings	No	26,644

Other Sites Where You Can Post Your Resume

America's Talent Bank

`http://atb.mesc.state.mi.us/`

This site is maintained by the U.S. Department of Labor, as a service to employers looking for talent. You enter your resume, or multiple resumes if you wish. Employers, when they come to this site, search all the resumes on this site by entering the skills wanted, or job title, or education, or location, or salary -- words selected from the same pre-defined list you were offered, in building your resume there. Currently only some States are connected to this Talent Bank; you can find out if your State is among them, by visiting the site, and clicking on "ATB Participating States" at the bottom of their home page. This site is a related, linked site to **America's Job Bank**. (Registration required.)

HeadHunter.NET

`http://www.HeadHunter.NET/`

Once you put your resume here, this site will automatically post your resume, either for free, or for a fee. Registration required.

The World Wide Web Employment Office

```
http://www.harbornet.com/biz/office/
annex.html
```

This resume site will post your resume as a Web page on its site (it'll cost you $35 for six months) or, if your resume is already up on a Web site or home page somewhere else, they will link to your resume for $10/yr. You will recall, if you've already been to the section on Job Posting Sites, that this site has links to countries all around the world, with employment opportunities organized by occupation (over 700 occupational fields, in fact) rather than by industry.

The Riley Guide

```
http://www.dbm.com/jobguide/resumes.html
```

Margaret Dikel (formerly Margaret Riley) has put together a superb list/chart of resume sites. Absolutely awesome! A major public service, updated to the minute.

JobBankUSA's List of Resume Usenet Newsgroups

```
http://www.jobbankusa.com/useresum.html
```

Leaving the Web, elsewhere on the Internet there are the USENET newsgroups where resumes can also be posted. Job Bank USA has a limited list of these, at the above site. Chief among them is **us.jobs.resumes**.

If you ever need to search for additional resume newsgroups on your own, there are five different queries you can enter in any newsgroup search engine. The first is "resumes", of course. The second is "jobs.wanted". The third is "requests for employment". The fourth is your geographic preference (e.g., Bay Area, or ba). And the last, when all else fails, is just the word "jobs."

Sites Where You Can Hide Your Identity

Let's say you're presently employed, and you don't want your employer to know that you are planning to leave, or maybe even just testing the waters of the job market. Or, let's say you don't want to get a lot of unwanted e-mail advertisements, in response to your online resume. There are Web sites which will post your resume but hide your identity, some for free, some for fee. If you think that because a site charges you a fee, it must be more effective, or more efficient, than one that is free, think again. Resume posting 'job banks' existed long before the Internet came along, and their history has always been the same: fee or free are equally long shots. Putting them online changes nothing.

Here are two examples of such sites, one free, one for-fee:

<u>BridgePath</u>

`http://www.bridgepath.com/`

This is a free resume site which allows job-hunters to hide their identity. It however, specializes in college graduates or people with less than twelve years' work experience. Here recruiters/employers, who have a job or internship they want to fill, come online to search through the 'bank' of those who previously signed up here by filling out a 10 minute online questionnaire, which keeps their identity hidden online. Recruiters can search by major field of study, industry, location, and more than 20 other criteria. When (and if) they find a candidate they like the sound of, BridgePath (not the employer) then sends an e-mail notifying said candidate of the job opportunity. At that point, the candidate decides whether to respond or stay anonymous -- by submitting, or not submitting, their resume to that recruiter or employer.

The site's idea is of course a good one; it is cousin to the idea I discuss below ('Search-While-You-Dream' Programs). Apropos of my comments there, the most recent time I visited BridgePath the statistics were: 150,000 students in their active database, but only 100 employers/recruiters a week searching that database.

ResumeBlaster

http://www.resumeblaster.com/

This is a for-fee resume site which also allows job-hunters to hide their identity. They charge $89 to send your resume anonymously to at least 783 recruiters; all personal information in your resume is suppressed, and you are given an anonymous e-mail address @resume-blaster.com, to which any recruiter interested in you must reply. Unless you then respond to that recruiter, your identity is never known.

'Search-While-You-Dream' Programs

You will note when you visit Web sites devoted to resumes, that an increasing number of them have a computer-program/'search-robot' that claims it "will do the job-hunting work for you." You register, give them some keywords, then go about your daily business knowing that they'll notify you by e-mail as soon as a job comes in, that matches your keywords. Resume sites have different names for the program (some call it a "personal search agent," others give it a *real cute* name -- Job Alert, etc.) but I think of them all as 'search-while-you-dream' programs.

Magazine and newspaper reviewers of such sites are enchanted by this idea of a job search-robot.

Of course job-hunters love the idea too: something keeping an eye out, on their behalf, for the jobs they're interested in.

As for me, I am in 100% agreement with the reviewers and the job-hunters: the *idea* is incredibly wonderful.

Unfortunately, the idea often leads nowhere. The math alone will tell you why. There are usually far more job-hunters registered on such a site for this kind of program, than there are ever job openings. And usually the

imbalance is huge. The chart (earlier) illustrated this well: Site A: 275,000 job-hunters, 25,000 job openings; Site B: 200,000 job-hunters, 10,000 job openings. Site C: 125,000 job-hunters, 4,000 job openings. You get the picture.

It's exactly like the lottery: somebody's gonna get chosen, and of course it could be you; but an awful lot of people are going to be left out in the cold, and they are never going to hear anything back. Zip. Zero. Nada.

So, never assume your job-hunting work is over just because you've registered in one of these search-robot programs, Don't ever sit at home, as an unemployed friend of mine once did, "waiting for God to prove He loves me, by sending a job walking in the door." (*God loved him so much He let him eventually go out and find the job for himself.*) Now that your resume's posted, now that you've registered with the search-robot, get out there and pound those pavements!! The life you save will be your own.

Do your homework on yourself first, then go visit any place that looks interesting to you, whether or not they are known to have a vacancy. Use your contacts to help you get in, to the places you really love.

If you try resume posting sites,
and they turn up nothing that interests you,
see page 175, or click here for:
"If You Strike Out, and Can't Find A Job"

3.
Career Counseling Sites

Subjects

in This Section on Career Counseling Sites

The Fairy Godmother Report on
Career Counseling Sites

Sites

in this section on Career Counseling Sites,
with Descriptions and Links

Carol Kleiman's Article   CareerPro

Keirsey Site   personalitytype.com

Resource Materials on TYPE

Description of the Enneagram

Enneagram Personality Dynamics

Enneagram: An Adventure in Self Discovery

Birkman "Career Style Summary™"

John Holland's SDS   The Career Interests Game

The Career Key   Creative Job Search Manual

Career Development Manual   Job Search Guide

Career Planning Process   The Riley Guide

Top Ten Jobs for People Who . . .

1998 Career Guide

Official Cool Jobs List   Backdoor Jobs

A Yellow Wood   Informational Interviewing

Careers.wsj.com

Best Online Articles about Interviewing

Kaplan's Careers In/Site

Virtual Interview   Tales from the Career Crypt

CareerMosaic Campus Directory

RPI Career Resource   JobSmart

About Work   The Career Action Center

Forty Plus

When things just aren't going well with your job-hunt, you may decide that something is wrong with the way you're going about it. That is a *great* realization, and not every job-hunter comes to it. If you do, you are a rare breed. Okay, so you realize you need a little career counseling, and you're hoping to find it on the Internet. This brings us to:

The
Fairy Godmother Report:
Career Counseling Sites

WHAT YOU'D HOPE TO FIND: Well of course, you'd hope the Internet would just tell you what you should do with the rest of your life. End of story. (That's what fairy godmothers are for!)

Getting a *little* more realistic, you'd hope to be able to find four career counseling things on the Internet:

(1) some decent interactive tests to give you a quick idea about a possible new career direction you might take; *plus*

(2) some articles dealing with various career issues, to further brush the cobwebs away from your thinking; *plus*

(3) longer career manuals for you to read when you have more time; *plus*

(4) FAQs (Frequently Asked Questions) dealing with common problems in the job-hunt. And each answer would be:

- given in some detail, running a couple of paragraphs or on up to a page;
- written by *truly competent* career-counselors;
- at no cost to the job-hunter; and without the career counselor or counseling center trying to sell additional services and products -- often *expensive* services (*hidden agendas*).

WHAT YOU ACTUALLY GET: Bingo! With career counseling you enter a job-hunting arena where the Internet comes close to giving you what you'd hope for. True, the Internet still cannot replace a live career counselor -- even if the Internet does have e-mail and chat rooms. But, so far as generic career counseling *without a human body* is concerned, you can indeed find much of what you'd hope to find on the Internet -- as outlined in the hopes above, except for "detailed answers to common job-hunting problems."

In that department, I must admit I am stupefied at some of the superficial (and 'dead wrong') advice that I sometimes read online about job-hunting, resumes, and the like. Of course, this defect would be cured real fast if these 'personnel experts' had to go out and find a job themselves tomorrow. But, that teeny-tiny objection aside, all the rest you'd hope for is here: tests, articles, manuals, FAQs. The whole works.

HOW EFFECTIVE? Well, there's only so much that impersonal online career counseling can do. Hence, my estimate of the effectiveness of Career Counseling sites on the Internet in getting you a job: **10 percent**. That is, out of every 100 people who seek out career counseling on the Internet, 10 of them will find a job thereby, with the aid of the coaching that they pick up there. I think 90 will need more help, or can do it without any help.

WORDS YOU'LL HAVE REASON TO REMEMBER: "Know then thyself; presume not the Web to scan, until you know what you love to do, and have evolved a plan." *(With apologies to Alexander Pope)*

Online Career Counseling: Free Interactive Tests

Many people like to take shortcuts. Shortcuts, that is, to finding out who they are and what they should do with their life.

Hence, the popularity of the interactive tests that are increasingly coming onto the Internet, mostly for free. If you like such tests then you may enjoy this collection -- and perhaps find some helpful clues about future directions for your life and your work.

Now to the tests. Interactive tests online divide into two categories: personality tests, and career or vocational tests -- though sometimes the line between them gets a little hazy. We will look at each category, in turn.

Free Online Tests Dealing with
Personality/ Traits

Most of the interactive tests/instruments/sorters that are on the Web are not career tests, strictly speaking. They are "personality tests/games/ instruments." But, as <u>Carol Kleiman</u> points out, it is important that your future job or career fit your personality; so, "personality" is not without career implications, at the very least.

http://cgi.chicago.tribune.com/career/
articles/kleiman/story/0,1697,
9802150119,00.html

Personality TYPE

These *instruments*, particularly the Myers-Briggs Type Indicator (MBTI), are beloved by many career counselors. Incidentally, "Type" means "what kind of personality do you have?" -- not "was this set in Courier or Palatino?" Anyhoo, the Myers-Briggs Type Indicator is not on the Internet. But three other tests, quizzes, or 'sorters,' dealing with "Personality Type" are.

<u>The Personality Page</u>

http://www.meyers-briggs.com/

This is the best of the three, in my opinion. It does not offer you the Myers-Briggs Type Indicator, but it does offer a test measuring your "Type" -- they call it "The Personality Questionnaire." They charge a fee for you to take this test online, but the charge is nominal ($3), and the results are quickly given. They then give you a lengthy summary, in MBTI language, of your Type, which you can print out. Also two other reports, on the implications of your Type for relationships, and on some suggested careers ("meant to be a starting place, rather than an exhaustive list . . ."). But the career report lists typical traits that you have to offer to employers, and the career suggestions are ranked, according to those careers which are most commonly chosen by your Type, on down to those least chosen. I like this site, a lot; their reports seem to me to be generally 'on target,' and the whole site is beautifully done.

The Keirsey Character Sorter and the Keirsey Temperament Sorter

http://www.keirsey.com/

Keirsey has a more extensive, but also more complicated, site. It has explanations of Personality Type, and lengthy descriptions of the various temperaments. It has two interactive tests/sorters: the Keirsey Character Sorter (which is newer and more complete), and the Keirsey Temperament Sorter (which is online in several languages -- English, Spanish, Portuguese, and German, currently). The site is interactive, and once you've answered its questions, it gives its results to you in *Myers-Briggs-Personality-Type language* ("you are an ENFP") -- with colored graphs. All to the good. The bad news is: you have to go to several places within the site, before you can find out what it all means, for you.

Resource Materials on Personality Types

```
http://sunsite.unc.edu/personality/
faq-mbti.html
```

If you want to learn more about Personality Types than is available online, the Resource Materials site has a very extensive bibliography of printed materials that you can go look for in your local library, or any bookstore (such as amazon.com or the one down on Main Street).

In my view, the fundamental defect of Personality Type instruments is that they are great at illuminating the *style* with which you do any job, but often misguided at predicting what career(s) that implies. I can tell you from decades of experience: dream jobs or careers are defined by much more than just 'Type' or "style." I would therefore take all Personality Type *career suggestions* with a huge grain of salt. But they may stimulate your own ideas, which is a very good thing. For that reason, they're sometimes well worth taking.

The Enneagram

This is another highly-popular test or instrument, these days, though how much it has to say about career-choice is also in wide debate. We can say this much: career choice is always a search for the self, and for work more fitting to that self. In this sense, the Enneagram at the very least has career *implications*, and is useful for stimulating self-awareness, self-observation and growth.

Sites dealing with it exist in a number of places on the Web. The three that I think are best, are:

A Brief Description of the Enneagram

```
http://www.freshy.com/personality/
enndesc.html
```

Ben Mitchell, of CompuServe UK, maintains a site called Personality Online (freshy.com), which has a very good basic introduction to the Enneagram, together with an interactive version of the test, that you can take. I like its layout, and its honesty ("The tests and information held on this site are in no way guaranteed to be correct or accurate.") This is my favorite among the three.

Enneagram Personality Dynamics

```
http://graphics.lcs.mit.edu/
~becca/enneagram/
```

Rebecca (Becca) Xiong of the MIT Laboratory for Computer Science, maintains another impressive site dealing with the Enneagram. For those who want to delve more deeply into the instrument and its philosophy, this is the answer to their prayers. Becca is very thorough. She offers an FAQ (Frequently Asked Questions), descriptions, diagrams, another version of the test that you can take interactively, an Enneagram chat room, a message board, and a list of some of the other sites on the Web that have to do with the Enneagram.

The Enneagram: An Adventure in Self Discovery

```
http://www.aa.net/gonw/enneagram/
ennea.htm
```

A site called "The Enneagram: An Adventure in Self Discovery," maintained by Jack High, a certified Helen

Palmer teacher who resides in the Northwestern U.S., has a most complete list of Enneagram resources, seminars, history, etc. This is for those who want to do further research into the whole idea of the Enneagram.

Free Online Tests
Dealing with Careers

We turn now from personality tests to career tests, also called vocational tests. Before you look at these, you should familiarize yourself with:

The Seven Rules About Taking Career Tests

1. **There is no one test that everyone loves.** To begin with, some people hate all tests. Period. End of story. Forcing these tests on your best friend (if they feel this way) could lead to your premature demise.

Other people like tests, but hate particular kinds of questions. For example, some people dislike "forced choice questions," where they must pick between two choices that are equally bad, in their view. Other people dislike "ranking yourself against others" questions, because, with their low self-esteem, they rank themselves poorly in comparison with "others" in almost everything. Other people don't like "pick occupations you like" questions, because they've learned by experience that all occupations as commonly practiced are a mixture of good and bad, and they keep thinking of the bad stuff, when each occupation is mentioned. Other people don't like questions about how they would behave in certain situations, because they tend to pick how they wish they behaved, rather than how in fact they actually do.

Hence, the *form* of a test has to feel right to the individual who is taking it. With tests, as with so many other things in life, "one man's meat is another man's poison."

2. **There is no one test that always gives better results than others.** You may take a test that gives you wonderful suggestions for future careers, but when you ask your best friend to take the same test, their results may be way off the mark -- and you are dismayed. Tests have personality -- and with respect to a given test, one person will love its look, feel, taste, and touch, while another person will hate it on sight. And, unfortunately, how one feels about a test will definitely skew the results.

3. **No test should necessarily be assumed to be accurate.** We turn to tests with the hope that someone can definitely tell us who we are and what we should do; and we think a test will do that. No, no, no. You can't say, "Well this must be who I am; the test says so." Test results are sometimes way off the mark. On many online (and offline) tests, if you answer even two questions inaccurately, you will get completely wrong results and recommendations. I know countless sad stories about people whose lives were sent down a completely wrong path by test 'results' that they believed when they shouldn't have. You should take all test results not with just a grain of salt, but with a barrel.

Tests have one great mission and purpose: to give you ideas you hadn't thought of, and suggestions worth following up. But if you ask them to do more than that, you're asking too much.

4. You should take several tests, rather than just one. You will get a much better picture of your preferences, profile, and good career suggestions from three or more tests, rather than just one. It's the old idea, since at least the time of the Second World War of 'triangulating' the source of a transmission. You need to 'triangulate' your test 'profiles,' in order to find your true self.

5. **Always let your intuition be your guide.** You know more about yourself than any test does, or ever could. Treat no test outcome as 'gospel'; reject the summary the test gives you, if it just seems dead wrong to you. Trust your intuition. On the other hand, if you really like the suggestions a test gives you, don't agonize about whether those suggestions are worth tracking down -- just do it. Always listen to your heart.

6. **Don't let tests make you forget that you are absolutely unique on the face of the earth -- as your fingerprints attest.** There is a sense in which all tests tend toward one unvarying result: because they deal in categories, they don't really tell you what's unique about you, but rather they tend to end up saying "you are an ENFP" or "you are an AES," or you are a "Blue." It's 'a category' they're talking about, but I like to think of it as 'a tribe' -- you are lumped with a lot of other people -- and sometimes it is even the wrong tribe.

Job expert Clara Horvath puts it well: career counseling at its best -- person to person, face to face -- treats you not as a member of some category or 'tribe' but as a unique job-seeker seeking to conduct a unique job-hunt, by identifying a unique career and then connecting with a unique company or organization, that you can uniquely help or serve.

7. **You are never finished with a test until you've done some good hard thinking about yourself.** Tests are fun, but just reading the results isn't enough. You're not done until you've thought hard about what distinguishes you from every other member of the human race, and makes you (like your fingerprints) unique. With *that* knowledge, you can then set out to find the work you were uniquely put here on earth to do, i.e., your unique mission in life. Without that hard thinking, tests become just "a flytrap for the lazy."

Now, to the free online career tests:

The Birkman Method

Birkman "Career Style Summary™"

```
http://www.review.com/birkman/
birkman.cfm
```

This is a 'forced choice' test, asking you for the most part to choose between two categories, even if you don't particularly like either one. If you don't like *forced choice* questions, you probably won't like this test.

I found myself liking this test a lot. A shortened version of "The Birkman Method,®" this little gem has three sterling virtues, in my view: it is fast, with only 24 questions to answer; secondly, the format is attractive, with a great use of color in both the display and the printout of its results (assuming you have a color monitor and color printer, of course); and thirdly, it often presents you with some really interesting career suggestions.

After you've answered the 24 questions, you will get a general description of your interests, skills, and preferred style (described in terms of the "Birkman Colors"), as well as a list of careers that all of this points to, chosen from a list in the Princeton Review's *Guide to Your Career*. Also, there's a detailed description of each career online, a starting point for any subsequent face-to-face exploration.

Like any test, this *can* lead you seriously astray, if you aren't scrupulously honest about your actual behavior. e.g., Do you really feel so patient, when you're kept waiting? Lie, and you'll deserve what you get. In any case, you should regard its findings as "possibilities" rather than "the gospel truth" about who you are. But, if you're puzzled about what career to choose next, this may give you some good ideas to explore further, matched to your skills and interests.

And speaking of ideas to explore, on the same site is a terrific list of <u>Top Ten Jobs for People Who. . . .</u> which you should also check out.

`http://www.review.com/career/topten.cfm`

John Holland's SDS (Self-Directed Search)

My favorite career system for two decades has been John Holland's RIASEC system, and its stepchild, your three-letter 'Holland Code,' which you determine by taking John Holland's *Self Directed Search* instrument. (There is an online version of the SDS at `http://www.self-directed-search.com,` which you can take (free) and then get a personalized report online, (for $7.95).

There are two unofficial free sites that also attempt to suggest what your 'Holland Code' might be:

The Career Interests Game

`http://www.missouri.edu/~cppcwww/`
`holland.shtml`

John Holland and I have been friends for the past 25 years, and many years ago in a playful moment I invented a brief, quick, hazy overview of his RIASEC system, based on my idea of someone walking into a room where a party was going on, and different groups (the RIASEC groups) were gathered in six separate corners of the room. It's called 'The 'Party Exercise' and it's in all my books as well as on the *Parachute CD-ROM,* but not (officially) on the Internet; however there is a version of it online, sans *title,* sans *diagram,* but with my wording, at the University of Missouri site. There they call it The Career Interests Game, and while it lacks my central graphic, they've otherwise done a great job of presenting the exercise in color, with career links, etc. It gives you a good 'first guess' at your three-letter 'Holland Code,' but recommends that you also take the paper version of John Holland's Self Directed Search test.

The Career Key

```
http://www2.ncsu.edu/unity/lockers/
users/l/lkj/
```

The Career Key, Lawrence Jones' interactive instrument, is a little longer test, also designed to tell you your "Holland Code." It's relatively brief to take -- though longer than The Career Interests Game -- and does well in giving you your three-letter 'Holland Code.' But, when it then offers you some possible occupations to consider, that match your Code, it is nowhere near as helpful as the Birkman. The reason is that occupations are organized here by 'single-letter-Holland-codes' rather than by 'three-letter-Holland-codes' -- to my mind, a serious defect. You are left to flounder around among all the "A" occupations or all the "R" occupations, rather than their using the second and third letters of your 'Holland code' to focus things down a bit, for you.

But, on the positive side, The Career Key nicely links

its list of occupations directly to the renowned Occupational Outlook Handbook *in its current edition*, and by clicking on any occupation in Career Key's list, you are taken to a detailed description of that occupation. A very nice touch.

Online Career Counseling:
Job-Hunting Manuals

There are job-hunting manuals -- of all sorts and de-scriptions -- everywhere on the Web, but these are my favorites -- my Parachute Picks:

<u>Creative Job Search</u>

http://www.des.state.mn.us/cjs/
cjs_site/cjsbook/contents.htm

This site, maintained by the Minnesota Department of Economic Security, has put together the equivalent of a job-search manual, on their "Creative Job Search" page. Mark this: these authors really understand what *skills* are (unusual, for the Internet). Employment applications, interviews, etc. are also covered.

<u>Career Development Manual</u>
<u>(Second Edition)</u>

http://www.adm.uwaterloo.ca/
infocecs/CRC/manual-home.html

The career center at the University of Waterloo has put together a thorough detailed manual to guide you through your job-hunt; its self-assessment section is one of the best on the Internet.

Job Search Guide:
Strategies for Professionals

http://atb.mesc.state.mi.us/atb/
text/guide/index.html

An amazingly thorough 74 page introduction to the job search, put out by the the United States Employment Service, is posted on this site; the manual can be printed out on your home printer.

Career Planning Process

http://www.cba.bgsu.edu/class/webclass/
nagye/career/process.html

A guide called "The Career Planning/Competency Model," authored by Pam Allen and Ellen Nagy, has a good list of transferable skills amidst its self-assessment exercises on this site, hosted by Bowling Green State University in Ohio.

If you want more than these four, visit the Riley Guide for additional suggestions, and links. This famous site on the Web has a good summary of the other job-search guides on the Internet.

The Riley Guide

http://www.dbm.com/jobguide/
jsguides.html

Online Career Counseling:
Job-Hunting Articles

All job-hunting articles divide into three basic categories: WHAT, WHERE, and HOW.

WHAT do you want to do?
WHERE do you want to do it? *And,*
HOW do you get hired there?

My Parachute Picks:

WHAT do you want to do?
Top Ten Jobs for People Who. . . .

http://www.review.com/career/topten.cfm

This is one of the great career lists on the Web. People who. . . . Like to Keep Learning; or. . . . Need to Pay Off Student Loans *Right Away;* or . . . Can't Stand Ties or Pantyhose; or . . . Have Type-A Personalities; or . . . Long for Unpredictable Days; or . . . Love People; or . . . Like to Work with Their Hands. That adds up to 70 jobs, actually, described here in great and helpful detail. (This is excerpted from *The Student Advantage Guide to Your Career,* by Alan B. Bernstein and Nicholas R. Schaffzin; Princeton Review Publishing, 1998.)

1998 Career Guide: Find Your Career

http://www.usnews.com/usnews/edu/
beyond/bccguide.htm

Written particularly for college students or would-be college students, this guide from *U.S. News and World*

Report lists "the hottest jobs of the year in 20 different fields" and has career outlooks for those jobs; also, it lists related job listing sites and associations, for each career. Very nice! This guide has a number of other interesting articles, such as "Job search on the Net," "part-time career paths" and "estimated starting salaries for graduates."

The Official Cool Jobs List

http://www.cooljobs.com/list.htm

If all the usual occupations leave you bored, here is a list (with examples) of jobs or careers that are *different*.

Backdoor Jobs

http://www.backdoorjobs.com/

If you're baffled as to a future career, and waiting for revelation from above, you could decide to 'play the field' with a short-term job, to explore *possibilities*. Voila! here is this site, by Michael Landes, precisely for those interested in short-term work experiences. The text here is actually a sampling from his book, *The Back Door Guide to Short Term Job Adventures;* but there are enough ideas about jobs and careers online for you to get some good clues. You may, of course, wind up saying to yourself "Well, I want more, so I guess I'm going to have to go buy his book." Don't worry; it's a good book.

A Yellow Wood: Diverging Career Pathways for Humanities PhDs

```
http://humanitas.ucsb.edu/depts/
english/altcareers/index.html
```

Actually, these articles aren't just for PhDs, but for anyone majoring in the humanities (or liberal arts) and wondering what on earth to do after graduation. It's a relatively new site created by students at UC Santa Barbara. Under the heading of "Travelogs" it's got an interesting series of articles by humanities majors about how they found their way into various industries (not predictable from their major). "Paths" links to job boards and job listings in non-academic career paths, while "Status Quo" has articles on the current and future state of the job market for humanities graduates. My favorite quote from this site: *"While there is considerable cause for optimism, the ability to tread water for another five years or so would help."*

For additional help with the WHAT question, look in the Research section of this Guide, under **Research Sites: Career Fields**.

WHERE do you want to do it?

Informational Interviewing

```
http://danenet.wicip.org/jets/
jet-9407-p.html
```

This important technique, serving as an alternative to the traditional job-hunt, is explained and discussed at this site; while they make the technique a bit more complex than it needs to be, this site still provides a good overview.

For additional help with the WHERE question, look in the Research section of this Guide, under **Research Sites: Geography** and **Research Sites: Identifying Companies in Your Field**.

HOW do you get hired there?

Careers.wsj.com

http://www.careers.wsj.com

Under the heading "Job-Hunting Advice," this site has quite a number of articles about the HOW: including how to react after losing one's job, plus other HOWs: making a career change, relocating, searching, networking, using resumes, and interviewing. While the articles are aimed at executives and management, their advice should be useful to all job-hunters. Taken from the *Wall Street Journal's* archives (among other places), these articles are on this relatively new site on the Web, under the leadership of Tony Lee, the former editor of *WSJ's National Business Employment Weekly. (The one negative: The way that frames are used on this site drives me nuts. Some other users of the site have reported a similar reaction. Hopefully, however, you will love them.)*

The Best Online Articles about Job Interviewing

http://www.golden.net/~archeus/
intres.htm#Articles2

Canadian author and job expert Gary Will has done a

marvelous job, not only of listing (and linking to) dozens of articles on the Web about interviewing; *but* of writing cogent and tremendously insightful reviews of each of those articles. A most impressive site; an even more impressive reviewer. I must confess I'd never even heard of Gary Will until I literally stumbled across this site, earlier this year; but having now studied what he's written, I find his evaluations are ones I agree with, his instincts are impressive, and his knowledge of online resources is encyclopedic. I think he's one of the best minds on the Web job-hunting sites.

Kaplan's Careers In/Site

http://www1.kaplan.com/view/
article/0,1275,536,00.html

This site has a number of (good) points about how to prepare for an interview, with practice questions, and special instructions about an interview that takes place in a "Restaurant Setting," not to mention what one should do after the interview -- all of which I agree with, heartily.

Virtual Interview

http://aboutwork.com/ace/virtual.html

This site, StudentCenter.com, has a famous 'virtual interview' exercise called "Ace the Interview." It gives you the opportunity to practice a hiring interview, by offering you questions with multiple choice answers, and then telling you whether or not you chose the best answer. If you did not, it gives you a chance to try and choose a better answer the second time around. Trouble is: while some of the questions are *cute*, in the case of the more serious questions, I didn't think any of the answers offered was the correct one to give! It needs: "None of the above" as an option. Oh well. Take it with a grain of salt, and enjoy.

"Tales from the Career Crypt"

`http://www.career-skills.com/tales.htm`

Finally, if after all the above reading (whew!) you're just in a mood for a good laugh or at least a smile, read these true stories by interviewers of job interviews that 'went South,' as we say up North. Sample: "Interrupted to phone his therapist for advice on answering specific interview questions."

For additional help with the HOW question, look in the Research section of this Guide, under **Research Sites: Geography** and **Research Sites: Salaries and Finances**.

For Further Help:
Career Counseling Offices

If the above tests, manuals and articles don't give you what you wanted in the way of career counseling, your life preserver could be the Career Offices on the Internet. There are two kinds:

College or University Career Offices, that have online presences -- often with useful job-hunting advice, and other materials; *and*

Non-profit or commercial Career Offices that are online.

College or University Career Offices Online

A number of sites list such offices, but I think the best lists are to be found at:

CareerMosaic Campus Directory

http://www.careermosaic.com/cm/
cc/cc8.html

It not only has a comprehensive list of American University and College Career Centers on the Web, but it also links to Canadian centers, and Worldwide centers -- plus, other people's lists, such as Peterson's. Very impressive.

RPI Career Resource

http://www.rpi.edu/dept/cdc/homepage.html

This site, maintained by Rensselaer Polytechnic Institute, has a good list of career counseling sites, at least for the U.S.

Nonprofit or Commercial Career Offices Online

Many of the famous commercial job listing sites on the Internet -- such as CareerMosaic -- function essentially as an Online Career Counseling Office, with other services besides job listings or resume postings. Go browse them, to see. My Parachute Picks from among nonprofit or commercial sites:

JobSmart

http://jobsmart.org/

Developed by job expert Mary-Ellen Mort, this is a *great* career counseling site, to my mind one of the three top job-related sites on the Web. While the focus of this site is California, it has many articles that apply to all job-hunters: a list of (and links to) online career guides, a truly great section on resumes, descriptions of the hidden job market, a place to write with your career counseling questions ("Ask Electra"), news of California job fairs and job hotlines, not to mention the best collection of salary surveys that exists on the Internet.

About Work

http://www.aboutwork.com/

This is a career counseling center that is just one part of a much larger network: *i*Village.com: The Women's Network, which its three founders created in order to build community. Of course it's designed for women, but 96% of all career advice is *gender-independent*, anyway. Click on "Career" on their home page, and Voila! you have access to *Tools* (e.g., "Assess Yourself"), *Features* (e.g., "Networking Center"), and *Resources* (e.g., "Job Listings"). They also will e-mail you their Career Newsletter. And they have a student center. To really use this site, you have to sign up first as a member, but it's free.

If you want a live chat, in real time, you can go to "Chat Central" and choose Career: Casual Chat, or Work from Home: Casual Chat. (They even instruct you as to how to talk to/type to the other people who are online at the same time as you.)

100

If you'd prefer a message board, where you can just leave a well-composed inquiry and have other people take a crack at answering it, there are a whole bunch of **Career** message boards that are (mercifully) grouped by job-hunting topic. Alternatively, if you'd prefer that 'an expert' answer your questions, they have a section called 'ask the experts' (there are five of them), with their own message boards where you can post your query and hope they answer it; they also have a weekly column, that each of them posts here. The last time I visited, one of the experts (Hope Dlugozima) was giving advice on how to get the attention of headhunters that was extremely sound, and well-informed. Unusual on the Web!

The Career Action Center

http://www.careeraction.org/

This Center, located at 10420 Bubb Road in Cupertino, California (in case you're in the vicinity), is one of the most famous career counseling places in the U.S. (they invented and trademarked the phrase Career Resilience™) and they have a great array of job-hunting helps for those who are members -- you can join online. But even non-members have access to a variety of career counseling articles on this site, including the wise "Gelatt's Guidelines to the Future" by career expert H.B. Gelatt -- who will enter into conversation with you about these ideas, via e-mail from this site.

Forty Plus

`http://www.fp.org/chapters.htm`

Here we go 'offline.' If you are over forty years of age, are 'a professional' and want to find a career counseling support group in your geographical area, this is a nice updated list of such support groups -- and where they are to be found, in major cities of the U.S. and Canada.

4.

Sites to Help Your Research

Subjects

in This Section on Research Sites

Finding Out More About the Company

A Guide to Researching Companies Well

What You Wish You Had Known

Resources for Those Seeking **Self Employment**

Resources for Those Seeking **Temp Work**

Resources for Those Interested in **Volunteering or Working for Nonprofits**

Resources on the Internet for **Minorities**

Resources for **Women**

Resources for **Gay and Lesbians**

Resources for **Elderly**

Resources for **People with Disabilities**

Research Sites: **Standard Reference Works**

If You Want Further Education or Training

Sites

in this section on Research Sites,
with Descriptions and Links

MetaCrawler   ALL-IN-ONE Search Page

Human Search   Search Engine Watch

The Best Places to Live in America 1998

Careers.wsj.com   Housing Opportunity Index

Chambers of Commerce

Maps On Us   FreeTrip's Auto Pilot

The Weather Channel   Realtor.com

HomeScout

1998–1999 Occupational Outlook

Bureau of Labor Statistics' Projections

continued

104

America's Career InfoNet
Business Job Finder   AT&T Category Index
What Can I Do With A Major In . . . ?
Career Links on the Internet   Library Guides
SmartCalc.com   JobSmart Salary Info
CareerBabe's Salary Sites
Careers.wsj.com: Salaries & Profiles
Wageweb   Pencom   Engineering Salaries
Web & Internet Salaries   Real Rate Survey
ASAE.Net   Yahoo! Professional Organizations
BigYellow   GTE SuperPages
SalesLeads USA   BigBook   Hello Yellow
Europages   Yahoo! Company Directories
HotBot: Business & Finance
Accufind   Competitive Intelligence—Get Smart!
American City Business Journals
Mansfield University   Starting Point
CompaniesOnline   Hoover's Online
Dun & Bradstreet   IBM InfoMarket
SalesLeads USA   100hot
Free Agent Nation   Backdoor Jobs
Inc. Online   Entrepreneur Magazine
Small Business Administration
Yahoo! Small Business Information
Business Resource Center
iVillage: Work from Home   Freelance Online
The Temp-orary Solution

105

Temporary Employment: An Overview

The Shorter Work Time Action Page

Contract Employee's Handbook

Temporary Relief   Temp 24-7

The Red Guide to Temp Agencies

Yahoo!s List of Temporary Agencies

Nonprofit Resources Catalog

Internet Nonprofit Center   Action without Borders

Argus Clearinghouse

Good Works   Essential Information

4Work   VJF Internet Resources for Minorities

Minorities' Job Bank   Black Collegian

Saludos Web Career Center   Beatrice's Web Guide

WWWomen   FeMiNa

Women's Wire   Connections   Advancing Women

Yahoo! Company Directories   Social Security

Employment Resources for People with Disabilities

The Job Accommodation Network: The ADA

WORKink   Merriam Webster

OneLook Dictionaries   Research-It!

Internet Public Library   Online Reference Works

Online Books Page   Learn2.com, the ability utility

Random Generator

amazon.com   bookworm

The Newsletter Library

Argus Clearinghouse: Education

Colleges & Careers

The
Fairy Godmother Report:
Research Sites

WHAT YOU'D HOPE TO FIND: You'd hope that the Internet would turn out to be your fairy godmother and give you the answer to any question you could think to ask -- and, do so in the twinkling of an eye.

WHAT YOU ACTUALLY GET: Well, research is one of those tasks for which the Internet was born. Often, the Internet is a researcher's dream: a worldwide library at your fingertips, that you can access anytime, day or night, in your frumpiest clothes, without ever leaving your apartment or home. Time and again you can turn up just exactly what you were looking for: information about geographical areas you'd like to move to, career fields, companies, the content of particular jobs, etc.

But (you knew there was going to be a *"but"*), the outcome of your research on the Internet is always uncertain. It's fifty-fifty you will find the information you're looking for; and fifty-fifty you won't. Even if you search for hours.

Reasons you can come up empty:

1. **A lot of the information you want just isn't on the Web.** For example, if you're researching large organizations, there's probably a lot of stuff on the Web about them. But if you're researching small organizations, say ones with five or less employees, there may be nothing on the Web about them, save their address and phone number. I repeat: a lot of information just isn't on the Web. Period.

2. **Even if it's on the Web, that doesn't mean you'll necessarily be able to find it.** Oh, in theory a behemoth search engine (like Lycos or AltaVista) can find anything that is on the Web, but that's only 'in theory.' In practice, a recent study concluded that there are over 320 million Web pages, and even the best search engines are acquainted with only 100 million of those pages. (I'll do the math for you: that means two-thirds of the Web is unknown to a given search engine.) If you want to find what's on the Web, you need to use a whole bunch of search engines (or a metasearch site, such as Meta-Crawler). And even then, it may be out there on the Web, but all search engines will strike out. "There could be any percentage of pages out there that nobody has actually accessed yet . . . huge numbers of pages existing in an electronic shadowland never seen by humans." *Steve Lawrence, co-author of the study published in* Science, *4/3/98, reported at* http://www.neci.nj.nec.com/ homepages/lawrence/websize.html

3. **Even if search engines turn up what you're looking for, they will also turn up a mountain of stuff you** *weren't*

looking for. That's because search engines look for literal words, not concepts *(e.g., if you look for information about a job as a "writer," the search engine may offer you information on being an "accountant" at an insurance company. And you think to yourself: "How did that happen?" Well, it happened because that company described itself on the Web as "one of the largest writers of insurance in America").* Because of this little, ahem, *quirk,* search engines will sometimes erroneously turn up so many sites or pages in answer to your query, that you will have a nervous breakdown just discarding the bad answers: *e.g., I tried one search engine (it was Infoseek Ultra) that encourages "questions in plain English" and in answer to my question, "How can I find meta-search engines?" it offered me 17,572,329 sites or pages, that it claimed were related to my query.* You can of course eliminate this kind of 'overwhelm' by using a search form with advanced features -- such as AltaVista's.

```
http://www.altavista.digital.com/
cgi-bin/query?pg=aq
```

4. Finally, to add insult to injury, **even if you do find the information you were seeking online, a lot of times you don't know whether to trust the information or not, because the date when the site was last updated was back when dinosaurs were still roaming the earth.** *It is to cry.*

HOW EFFECTIVE? How helpful, or effective, then, is online research toward getting you a job? Well, **that depends** of course on what kind of information you're looking for, how essential it is for your job-hunt or career-change, and whether you score or strike out. In other words, the effectiveness rate is very 'situational.'

WORDS YOU'LL HAVE REASON TO REMEMBER:
Research on the Internet is always risk; always, adventure. Sometimes you soar; sometimes, you crash and burn. It is important to remember that the Internet is only one of the places for you to do research. Don't persist too long in any query here. *Sometimes your friend Eric or Erica could tell you in five minutes what you've spent three hours on the Web trying to find out, in vain.*

Research Sites: Search Engines

Lists have been our obsession elsewhere in this guide, but when it comes to research, there are so many topics you could research in the course of your job-hunt, so many sites to sift through for those topics, so much change happening all the time on the Web, that as Internet expert Mary-Ellen Mort puts it, "Researching the Web is like trying to research a mudslide."

Therefore, when it comes to doing research on the Internet, a search engine is going to be your best friend. Ah, but the question is, *"Which search engine?"* As described above, search engines differ greatly, in how much they know, and how they've organized it. What's a body to do?

I found that with a given query of mine, one search engine would know where the information was, on the Web; but with my next question, it wouldn't know anything, while another search engine would. So, I used to limp from search engine to search engine, trying to find which one knew anything, related to my query.

I used to, that is, until I discovered MetaCrawler and ALL-IN-ONE. Now, I never use anything else but these. Hence, they are my favorites -- my Parachute Picks:

MetaCrawler

`http://www.metacrawler.com/`

MetaCrawler sends your query to a number of search engines simultaneously: (AltaVista, Excite, Infoseek, Lycos, WebCrawler, LookSmart, The Mining Co., Thunderstone and Yahoo, currently).

There are, to be sure, other 'metasearch sites or engines' *(e.g., SavvySearch, Cyber 411, Dogpile, MetaFind, Profusion, Highway 61, Inference, Find, search.onramp.net, Mamma)* -- I've tried them all, but I infinitely prefer MetaCrawler over the others, for several reasons:

1. It's vastly improved -- in speed and everything -- since a company named go2net,Inc. (with its deeper pockets) took it over in February of 1997. Prior to that, I used to despair of it, more than once. But now:

2. MetaCrawler always displays its home page quickly, compared to other metasearch sites. In fact, it's gotten faster just in the past two months.

3. It makes it easy to choose "as a phrase" as your search condition (something you will need often -- e.g., if you're searching for something like "salary negotiation techniques").

4. It sometimes tells you what it's doing as it assembles the results.

5. It throws out duplicates, and ranks those that are left in order of relevance.

6. It is quick to display these ranked results (in seconds, not minutes), with good descriptions of same.

Because it builds on the strengths of a number of search engines, and in a synergistic way, I think it is definitely the most helpful search engine/site on the Web. I use it for everything.

Incidentally, on its home page you can choose to launch "MiniCrawler" which leaves the search engine in a separate little window on your screen at all times. Nice feature!!

ALL-IN-ONE Search Page

```
http://www.albany.net/allinone/
all1www.html
```

If MetaCrawler turns up nothing, ALL-IN-ONE could be your lifesaver. It is very impressive. All on one page, according to subject (Web, General Interest, Special Interest, etc.) this site lists more than 100 search engines, ready to serve you right on that page. The search engines listed here cover the Web, FTP, ListServers, USENET Newsgroups, Gopher, TELNET, Newspapers, Vendors, E-mail addresses, White pages, Yellow pages, Telephone numbers, Last names, Mailing Lists, Classifieds, Domain Names. The list is so extensive, and some of the search engines so highly specialized, that if what you're looking for has been cataloged by anyone on the Internet, you should be able to find it with one of these tools. The site was created by William D. Cross, and he keeps it very up-to-date (i.e., William even knows if some specialized search engine 'died' or moved to another

URL since last month -- Intellimatch, for example). The only downside of this site: the home page, while pretty, is sometimes quite hard to read -- light print against a dark background.

Human Search

http://www.humansearch.com/

If there's some piece of information you're desperate to find, and you think it should be on the Internet, there is a search site with actual human researchers, who will help you find the information you want, often within 48 hours -- for only $8.00. When I visited the site, they weren't accepting any more questions for the next three hours; so, be prepared to be persistent. They also have an archive (called Proteus) that will tell you answers to questions that have been previously asked.

Now, if you want more information about search engines in general, or in detail, the best site (and the only site) to visit is:

Search Engine Watch

http://www.searchenginewatch.com/

Danny Sullivan, the editor of this site, has an encyclopedic knowledge of all the search engines. He'll tell you their history, their statistics, which ones do better, in a variety of subject areas; and he'll also give you tutorials on how to use the search engines or how to improve your use of their search capabilities. See particularly the

"Search Engine Reviews Chart," to see which search engines have been rated highest. Outstanding site!

How Long Should You Search?

Be aware before you start using these search engines that, when you're doing research on the Internet, you can find so many interesting sidepaths that it can divert you from your job-hunt or career-change for weeks, *all the while giving you the illusion that you are hard at work on it.* "Hey, what do you mean I'm not working very hard on my job-hunt? I spent three hours yesterday surfin' the Net."

So, if you're going to do any of your research on the Internet, bring car-loads of self-discipline. I mean: *car-loads.* Know exactly what it is you want to know (write it out, on a piece of paper . . . please!). Go find that, write down the answer. Don't spend more than a predetermined amount of time trying to find that answer on the

Internet. Then, give up. Do that research in other ways than from your computer.

Cutting Your Search Time Down

If you use the search engines mentioned above, you will eventually come across some very useful sites. But since my desire is to cut your search time way down, in certain key arenas, let me suggest my Parachute Picks of sites that a job-hunter may find especially useful when doing research on the Internet:

Research Sites: Geography

The traditional three secrets to retailers' success -- location, location, location -- are the secrets of a job-hunt as well. Geographic focus, when looking for a job, when posting your resume, or when doing research, is key to your success.

You can research any place in the country, or the world, simply by typing its name into your favorite search engine's Query Box, together with any additional words you want to use in order to narrow that search, then hitting the Search button, and seeing what turns up. Also, general sites dealing with geography abound; here are my Parachute Picks:

The Best Places to Live in America 1998

```
http://pathfinder.com/money/
best-cities-97/
```

Want to move to a new city or town or country place? Wonder which one is best for you? *Money* magazine's site, here, not only has the top 300 cities -- according to their 11th annual reader survey -- but also a wonderful interactive feature called: "Find the best city for you." You rank nine criteria by how important they are to you, and then their search engine will tell you which cities (or places) fit the criteria as you ranked them. You can specify how many cities you want, and they'll give you the answers ranked and with data about the place, including a "cost of living comparator" (courtesy of home-fair.com) to help you figure out whether you'll be richer or poorer if you move from where you are. If you get too many choices, you can further refine it by ranking a list of 63 factors; however, the more factors you check, the more you risk the chance of finding out there's no place in the country like *that*. Wait for Heaven.

Careers.wsj.com

http://www.careers.wsj.com

Want to move primarily for the sake of finding a job, and you wonder where the unemployment is so low that finding a job *should be* a cinch? This site lists in a nice 'table' precisely which U.S. communities had the lowest (and highest) unemployment rates in a recent month (lowest was 1.6%, highest was 18.9% when I last visited -- ouch!). To get to the table (follow closely now): from the home page choose the section called **Salaries & Profiles**, and once there choose Career Indicators, once there scroll down and you should find the list. *(If you* *don't, please notify me by e-mail.)* Do remember that low unemployment for the town doesn't necessarily mean low unemployment in your field. Maybe they don't even have your field in that town (restaurants, gas stations, stores and the like, excepted).

Housing Opportunity Index

`http://www.nahb.com/mandl.html`

Want to move primarily for the sake of finding cheaper housing and thus being able to live on a smaller budget? Here's the latest quarterly survey of which areas in the U.S. have the least expensive housing (not to mention the most). Scroll down to the bottom of the page for further listings. (All dollar figures are in thousands, incidentally.)

Chamber of Commerce Directory

`http://clickcity.com/index2.htm`

Found a city or town (anywhere in the world) that you like the sound of, and want to know more about? Here is a directory of city/town chambers of commerce, plus a directory of cities-states-provinces, around the world -- with hotlinks to their Web sites and e-mail addresses. *Chambers of commerce for information about a city! Of course! What a great idea!*

In some cases, however, the implementation of the idea left a lot to be desired. Under 'chambers,' I sometimes got only their street address and phone number (the phone number was outdated, in one case). Under the cities-states-provinces, I sometimes found they had no information on some rather well known towns, like Walnut Creek, California. On the positive side, if they did list a city, they *sometimes* had quite a few job listings for that city, on their Employment resource board, which they had culled from various local job sites. Of course, so does that city's local newspaper (see <u>American Journalism Review NewsLink</u>).

```
http://www.newslink.org/news.html
```

As I said in the introduction to this section, when you want to know more about a town or city, go simple: try just typing its name into <u>MetaCrawler</u>, and see what turns up. Many towns and cities now have their own site with extensive information: e.g., Walnut Creek, California, at:

```
http://www.ci.walnut-creek.ca.us/
```

<u>Maps On Us</u>

```
http://www.mapsonus.com/
```

<u>FreeTrip's AutoPilot</u>

```
http://www.freetrip.com/
```

Decided to go visit the town or city in question? Decided to drive there? These two sites together will give you directions, a personal and comprehensive driving itinerary, total trip distance, driving time, location of hotels/motels, restaurants, tourist attractions along the way, and a whole series of detailed Maps right up to the door of your destination, etc.

My preference is Maps on Us, as I'm a visualist, but AutoPilot is helpful if you prefer written directions. In the end, I plot a trip with both of them, as each has some features the other doesn't. Together, they make one united right brain/left brain. A great use of the Web!

The Weather Channel

`http://www.weather.com/travel/index.html`

Decided to go visit the town or city in question? Decided to fly there? This will tell you what the weather will be like when you get there, and whether or not your flight will be delayed (applies to domestic flights only). They will also give you maps of the major roadways surrounding the airport.

Realtor.com

`http://www.realtor.com/`

If you've decided you might actually like to move to this town or city you've been exploring, this is a tremendously useful site. You will find here, *under the home page heading of "Movers Toolkit,"* a suite of very useful tools: The Salary Calculator (comparing cost of living between different cities), The Moving Calculator (to estimate interstate moving costs), The Insurance Professor (estimating auto and home insurance premiums in a new city), Relocation Crime Lab (giving you crime indexes for over 500 cities), a Mortgage Qualification Calculator (computing the loan amount for which you may qualify) and a Relocation Wizard (creating a timeline for your move). Realtor.com also has the largest number of home listings on the Web (over a million) -- though it doesn't cover all geographical areas, unfortunately. And, like many real estate sites on the Web, you have to go through several steps to get to where you want to be (some shortcuts would be nice . . . someday). Find a home you like, it will draw a map of the house's location for you, showing also the location of the nearest schools.

Home Scout

http://www.homescout.com/

If you're looking for a home, and you're not happy with the listings on the previous site, this site will give you many more listings indeed! It searches hundreds of independent listing Web sites for you, and displays the results very quickly. Their home page is their search page; I was impressed with the number of listings it turned up (80) for the small town I chose as guinea pig.

Research Sites: Career Fields

The 1998–99 Occupational Outlook Handbook

http://stats.bls.gov/ocohome.htm

This is the place to begin, *of course,* in researching particular occupational fields. It is the Bureau of Labor Statistics' official handbook.

Bureau of Labor Statistics' Projections

http://stats.bls.gov/news.release/
ecopro.toc.htm

You may wish to supplement the Outlook Handbook with figures and articles concerning the projected future of particular occupations. In that case, this is the site to visit.

America's Career InfoNet

http://www.acinet.org/

Here you can find information about particular occupations (training, outlook, earnings); particular geographic areas (demographic information), trends, and resources. You can search by "Menu," "Keywords," or "SIC Codes." The site is in a preliminary stage of development (their words), but already the information displayed is very helpful.

Business Job Finder

http://www.cob.ohio-state.edu/dept/
fin/osujobs.htm

Here you can find information about particular *business* careers, or careers in finance, accounting, or management, in its "Business Job Finder" maintained by The Fisher College of Business at Ohio State.

AT&T Toll-Free Internet Directory Category Index

http://www.tollfree.att.net/catnav.html

If the above lists don't give you enough ideas about possible fields, and you want more choices, there is another way to look for fields -- and that is, by going through the Yellow Pages and looking at the Yellow Page *categories.* Such categories are roughly equivalent to 'fields.' You can find them at this site. (Under each letter of the alphabet, you'll have to click on one to eight pages.)

What Can I Do With A Major In . . . ?

```
gopher://gopher.wustl.edu:70/11/
WU_Links/Career_Center/majchoose/major/
```

Washington University has put up an interesting site for majors in the classics, archaeology, English, fine arts, history, philosophy, and a number of other fields, indicating what kinds of jobs people with these majors wound up in. Food for thought.

Career Links on the Internet

```
http://www.rpi.edu/dept/cdc/
```

College students who want to know what to do with their major, once they've graduated, can find a list of (and links to) sites dealing with career choices upon graduation.

Library Guides

```
http://www.bradley.edu/irt/lib/
services/access/
```

Should you wish to learn more about a particular field off the Internet, by actually reading books, there's a great list of basic books to master for a whole series of fields, under the heading here of "Guides to Subjects," and "All Guides Alphabetically."

See also, related articles about "hot jobs" in the Career Counseling section of this Guide: Articles About Job-Hunting, What do you want to do?

Research Sites: Salaries and Finances

SmartCalc.com

```
http://www.smartcalc.com/SmartCalc/
docs/calclist.htm
```

I find this a very impressive site; it features dozens of online calculators, dealing with a multitude of financial questions: how much am I spending? how much can I borrow? how much will I save if I live on a budget? should my spouse work too? what car can I afford? how much will it cost to raise a child? what will it take to save for a college education? how much life insurance do I need? is a Roth IRA good for me? what will my expenses be after I retire? and many others. All forms are interactive calculators. Very useful tools to use before you approach salary questions in your current job-hunt.

General Collections:

JobSmart Salary Info

```
http://jobsmart.org/tools/salary/
sal-prof.htm
```

This is the best list of salary surveys on the Net (hands down!); other sites claiming to have big salary surveys actually just link to this one, the Mother of all salary surveys -- over 200 of them! Before you choose a career, before you hunt for a job, before you go in for the hiring interview, you'd better know this information!

CareerBabe's Salary Sites

http://www.careerbabe.com/
salarysites.html

This list overlaps JobSmart's in many respects, but it does have some novel lists of its own (salaries of men vs. women, etc.) It's well worth looking at, if JobSmart didn't give you enough to satisfy you.

Careers.wsj.com

http://www.careers.wsj.com/

On one part of this site, called **Salaries & Profiles**, they have another helpful collection of Salary Tables, for various professionals.

What distinguishes this site from the other salary sites is the fact that it displays the latest news about salaries and salary trends in various segments of the job market, culled from the *Wall Street Journal* daily and the *National Business Employment Weekly*. These articles are very current *and also* 'very archived' for quite some time back. Browse to see if your field has been in the news. A great service.

Specialized Collections:

Wageweb Salary Survey Data Online

http://www.wageweb.com/index.html

For those interested in HR salaries, Administrative salaries, Finance salaries, Information Management salaries, Engineering salaries, Healthcare salaries, Sales/Marketing salaries, or Manufacturing salaries, here are over 150 benchmark positions in those industries, updated recently. They tell you the 'mean' average salary, average minimum salary, average maximum salary, plus how many companies and employees are the basis for each figure (great information!).

Pencom Interactive Career Center

http://www.pencomsi.com/careerhome.html

This site also deals with salary research. It offers an interactive salary guide for those in high tech jobs in various settings (including academia and the military). The site has other 'goodies': some nationwide job listings, plus articles on particular careers.

The Engineering Specific Career Planning

http://ecn.purdue.edu/ESCAPE/stats/
stat_gifs/start_sals.html

This has a comparison of the starting salaries of various types of engineers (Purdue B.S. Graduates 1997). Chemical is the best paid; civil the least -- comparatively

speaking, of course. They also have 1997 salaries relative to how many years have elapsed since graduation.
```
http://ecn.purdue.edu/ESCAPE/stats/
stat_gifs/salary_d.html
```

Web and Internet Salaries
```
http://web1.aeanet.org/homepage/
pressrel/225a.html
```

For those toying with the idea of working in 'the Web industry' or other jobs connected to the Internet, this is the first-ever salary survey (4/20/98) of the 'top' Web positions, plus a description of what those positions involve -- in case you're attracted to the field.

The Real Rate Survey
```
http://www.realrates.com/survey.htm
```

On this bulletin board, "Computer consultants" (very broadly defined) post what they really made on their last job or contract, and where that was. You can search this completely-up-to-date site -- by salary, location, platform, etc. A great use of the Web, this site is maintained by Janet Ruhl, author of *The Computer Consultant's Workbook*. My only wish: that the info was displayed better, in real tables. The display tables were misaligned on both my screen and printer (and maybe on yours as well), but I reckon if the information is important to you, you'll make sense out of it!

Research Sites: Identifying Companies in Your Field

Once you've identified a field that interests you, you want to gain news about that field or industry, discover industry trends, pay scales for that profession, names of associations in that field, schedule of meetings or networking events, prospective employers, job listings, and the like. Begin with associations:

American Society of Association Executives

```
http://www.asaenet.org/
```

If you want to find out more information about a particular field (or fields), this site will give you a list of associations that are online, as well as those that aren't.

Yahoo! Professional Organizations

```
http://www.yahoo.com/Economy/
Organizations/Professional/
```

If you want to find out more information about a particular field (or fields), you want to go to their *Associations, or Professional Associations*, and many such associations (though not all) are listed here, together with a Search form.

Next, you will want to discover what companies, organizations, or businesses are in the field you've chosen, and in the geographical area where you would like to work.

On or off the Internet, your best bet for this task is always the Yellow Pages. There are at least five North American Yellow Pages sites on the Web that are nationwide -- BigYellow, BigBook, GTE Superpages, and American Yellow Pages, for the U.S., and Hello Yellow for Canada. There are regional Yellow Pages, as well, such as -- in the U.S. -- BayAreaYellowPages.com. And there are those which fall in between: they call themselves national, but seem more regional when you search, such as US*West* Dex Yellow Pages.

The five North American Yellow Pages sites that are nationwide offer incomplete listings. They are -- surprisingly -- not a reproduction of the complete Yellow Pages Phone Book you have sitting on your desk. They offer you only a "selection" from that Book, as I found out by slow and painful comparison checking.

Keep in mind: your Phone Book knows more than the Internet Yellow Pages do, about how many individual businesses there are in your chosen category if the town is nearby. Use that Phone Book at your elbow, if you're searching for local listings. The Internet will of course be helpful for places far away, that your phone book doesn't cover -- so long as you remember it's not going to give you a complete listing of businesses elsewhere. If you're going to use these directories, my advice is: start broad (geographically speaking), search all related categories on their lists, and of course leave "Business Name" blank.

Anyway, here are the strengths and weaknesses of the five national Yellow Pages sites on the Web:

BigYellow

http://www.bigyellow.com/cat_a.mat

This is Bell Atlantic's version of the Yellow Pages, and people will tell you this is the premiere Internet phone directory, with over 16 million business listings nationwide. If it's "business categories" you're looking for, it certainly is premiere; it has a list of over 7,000 categories for businesses -- (scroll down the page and you'll see the list, OR click on one of the letters of the alphabet, there). You can then search for what businesses there are in the category you have chosen, by town or city. You can also do a more complex geographical search, on up to a whole Metro Area, or suburban area, and on down to a neighborhood, or street!

But I found BigYellow's search engine to be very jumpy: when I asked for information about a business category in a nearby California town, it correctly displayed the name of the town I asked for, but then proceeded to give me the name of only one business -- and that was in Sterling, Virginia, 3,000 miles away! My dog-eared local phone book had the names of 22 businesses in that California town, in the identical category!

GTE SuperPages

http://superpages.gte.net/

This is GTE's version of the yellow pages. It lists "Top Categories," though not as many as BigYellow (above). Its listings were also very limited compared to my local phone book.

SalesLeads USA: American Yellow Pages

http://www.infoUSA.com/

This site, sponsored by infoUSA Inc., formerly named American Business Information, Inc., lists 11 million businesses (and 110 million households). From their home page, click on "American Yellow Pages," to get to their phone book by that name. You can search by "type of business" anywhere in the country, by town and state, using the category titles that you find in your own local yellow pages. Their listings, in the categories I tested, were as good as, or better than, those on any of the other four yellow pages sites. Plus, they give you a map as to where the business is located, and (for $5) a profile of the company or organization. My local phone book still knows more than they know. But among the Yellow Pages sites on the Internet, I think this one is the best.

BigBook

http://www.bigbook.com/

Hello Yellow

http://www.canada.com/helloyellow/

The various online Yellow Pages seem to me to be very 'intertwined.' BigBook, for example, is 'powered' by GTE Superpages (above). And both of these sites also use the database of infoUSA Inc. (see SalesLeads USA, above).

BigBook will give you all that it has for the U.S. It bills itself as "a whole new kind of Yellow Pages," but I found its categories confusing, and its listings quite off the mark, for the categories I tried; i.e., it failed to list one single company under the business category I chose for a nearby town, while my poor dog-eared phone book had many businesses listed in that identical category. On the plus side, BigBook will give you maps and driving directions.

Hello Yellow will give you all that it has for Canada. You can search by City, Province, Type of Business, or Name of Business.

Europages, The European Business Directory

http://www.europages.com/

For those looking for work in Europe, this site has 500,000 company addresses from over 30 European countries, with links to each country's Yellow Pages. You can search by country, subject, company name, etc. It also has a list (with links) to other sites that have economic data about Europe.

Beyond Yellow Pages, displayed or printed, where else do you look to find out what businesses there are in your chosen occupational category? Well, there are business directories, and a number of search sites have an index of them, together with links. My Parachute Picks are:

Yahoo! Company Directories

http://www.yahoo.com/Business_and_ Economy/Companies/

Yahoo has the most impressive list of directories that I've seen anywhere; this is the place where I would start if I were job-hunting tomorrow, and wanted to go beyond the phone book. Browse this index -- you'll find resources for women, minorities, gays/lesbians, and others. Choose "Directories" to get a list of (and links to) over 300 directories.

HotBot: Business & Finance

http://www.looksmart.com/ r?comefrom=ize-e65300&ize&e65300

According to a recent survey, HotBot has a larger knowledge of the Web (even so, that's only 34%) than any other single search engine -- *metasearch sites excepted.* Notwithstanding this, I think Yahoo!'s list is larger and better organized.

Accufind

http://www.nln.com/

From the home page, click on "Business." This will take you to Accufind's "Business/Corporate Resource

Sites" where a whole bunch of directories is listed, with links: including Home Based Businesses, Franchises, etc.

Research Sites: Finding Out More About the Company

Once you know the name of an organization or company that looks interesting, you'll of course want to be able to research it, and find out as much about them as you possibly can, before you ever go there for an interview. We'll call this 'preliminary research.' In the interview itself, you want to continue the research by asking intelligent questions *after* the interviewer has asked their own questions of you.

Okay, then, for this preliminary research online, here are my favorites -- my Parachute Picks:

Competitive Intelligence–Get Smart!

http://www.fastcompany.com/online/14/
intelligence.html

This is an introductory article about what business types can learn about rivals by skimming the Net -- but job-hunters will find helpful its principles about how to find out more about companies that interest you. *(Incidentally, this is on the site of a magazine -- Fast Company -- that is commanding a lot of interest among human resources professionals these days.)*

American City Business Journals

http://www.amcity.com/

Under the title of "**Back Issues** Search for . . ." this site will simultaneously search all its archives (of 39 weekly Business Journals, for various cities around the U.S.) for any mention of whatever company or organization you are interested in. There are other 'goodies' on this site, as well.

Mansfield U. Business/Economics Reference

http://www.mnsfld.edu/depts/lib/
mu-biz.html

To get you started, Mansfield University's Library online has a wonderful collection of *Business and Economics References* - - Business Yellow Pages, Canadian Statistics, Hoover's, EDGAR (SEC database), etc. This is like having a whole library at your fingertips! Surely somewhere here lies a directory that you will find helpful.

Starting Point-Business

http://www.stpt.com/busine.html

Starting Point has a great collection of Commercial Directories at this site. It also has "Business Power Search Sites" -- entrepreneurship, Chambers of Commerce (international), marketing and demographics data, SBA (Small Business Administration), updates on corporate activities, training and seminar locations, BigBook and more -- all searchable with but one entry on their search page!

CompaniesOnline

http://www.companiesOnline.com/

On this site you can search for information on over 100,000 public and private companies: you can register for free, and then they will tell you the annual sales, employee size, trade name, immediate parent, ultimate parent, contact name, contact title, e-mail, and location type, ownership structure, Web & e-mail addresses, and much more, for a particular company, if they have it. So far so good. On the downside: remember, there are 16,000,000 employers 'out there,' so only .6% are covered here, which means of course that 99.4% of all employers are missing here. If you're interested in one of the ones they do have, you'll of course be grateful for this site; but with many businesses, you will strike out again and again, as I did when visiting. The site is co-sponsored by Dun & Bradstreet, and Lycos, Inc.

Hoover's Online

http://www.hoovers.com

This is a relatively new site, founded by Hoover's -- a very respected name in the directory world. On this site, they have 3,000 Company Profiles, 10,000 Company Financial Reports, and 12,000 Company Capsules (brief overview, Web sites, and links) available to subscribers. Job-hunters get a free trial subscription. But here only .07% of all employers are covered, which means of course that 99.93% of all employers are missing here. If you're interested in one of the 12,000 they do have, you'll of course be grateful for this site; but with most small businesses, you will strike out again and again, as I did.

Other sites which have information about companies -- but will charge you for it -- are:

Dun & Bradstreet

```
http://www.dbisna.com/dbis/dnbhome.htm
http://www.dbisna.com/industry/
pindustry1.htm
```

Well of course Dun & Bradstreet has information about companies, more than 11 million of them. Click on "Reference and Research." If you want anything very detailed, those reports will cost you $20 or so. This site also has industry studies links to CompaniesOnline (above).

IBM InfoMarket

```
http://www.infomkt.ibm.com/
```

If you're looking for information about a smaller organization, this site can be a lifesaver! This site has a powerful search engine. When you can't find a company on any of the above sites, enter its name here, click on "Directories," and frequently they will find it for you, together with which Information Source has a report on that company or organization. Click again, and you can order the report immediately (for a fee, sometimes as small as 75 cents). You do have to be a registered user first, however.

Note: when you register, InfoMarket requires that you give them permission to share your user information with any Information Source they refer you to *and* (if you don't check the "Opt Out" box on the Registration page) to share that personal information with other (unnamed) third parties. If you don't want that kind of use of your personal information, be sure to check that "Opt Out" box!

SalesLeads USA

http://www.infoUSA.com/

If you want a report about smaller companies, this site, mentioned earlier, lists 100 million households and 10 million businesses. Click on "American Yellow Pages." Go through the search form. Once you find a business that interests you, they give you a map as to where the business is located, and (for $5, by using your credit card on the Secure Commerce Server on this site) you can immediately get a profile of the company or organization. The reports on the companies I checked were somewhat elementary but helpful and current: key executives, number of employees, estimated annual sales, credit rating code, other lines of business, and fax numbers. (Incidentally, this database appears to be one of the directories used in the IBM InfoMarket above. If you've been there, you may not need to come here -- except for the maps, of course.)

100hot

```
http://www.100hot.com/f500/
fullscreen.html
```

If you're looking for information about a larger corporation, this site lists and ranks its idea of the 100 top corporate sites belonging to the Fortune 500. Those corporate Web sites, of course, have information about that corporation -- maybe not quite what you wanted to know, but it's a start.

A Guide to Researching Companies Well

Having listed the sites, we come to the $64,000 question: exactly why should you be trying to research an organization? Two good reasons spring to the fore:

(1) First of all, you research an organization as a way of reassuring the interviewer that you cared enough to learn something about them, before coming in for the interview. This involves research at its most basic level -- their primary business, address, number of employees, etc. And the Internet can help with this basic sort of research -- in the case of many companies, but certainly not all.

(2) More importantly, you are also researching a company in order to protect yourself from making a horrible mistake -- ignorantly taking a job that you'll soon have to quit, because of something important about them, that you didn't know or bother to find out, before you started there. The purpose of this sort of research is to find that out ahead of time, before you take the job. (So that you won't take it!)

In such a case, what do you want to know? Well, think of the jobs you've had in the past, and try to recall the moment when you were about to leave that job -- your decision or theirs. What is it, at that moment, you wish you had known before you took the job? This will give you your research topics. Items which suggest themselves are such things as:

You wish you had known:
What the real goals of the place were, instead of the folderol they put in their annual report.
You wish you had known:
What 'the corporate culture' was like, there: cold and clammy, or warm and appreciative.
You wish you had known:
What kinds of timelines they conducted their work under, and whether they were flexible or inflexible.
You wish you had known:
What the job was really like.
You wish you had known:
Whether the skills you care the most about, in yourself, would really get used. Or was all that talk about 'your skills' just window dressing to lure you there -- and you, with rich people skills, ended up spending your time pushing paper?
You wish you had known:
More about the boss, and what she or he was like, to work for. Ditto for your immediate supervisor(s).
You wish you had known:
What your co-workers were like: easy to get along with, or difficult? And who was which?

You wish you had known:
How close the company or organization was to having to lay off people, or on how tight a budget they were going to ask your department to operate.

So, if that's your past, that's also your future: that's what you want to know about an organization that interests you, that's what you want to research before you get a job offer there (if you get a job offer there).

Can the Internet help with this kind of research? Well, if the Internet were loaded with chat rooms, filled with ex-employees of that organization, who were in a tremendously indiscreet (or anonymous) mood, you would indeed be able to research these things online.

And in fact, if it's a really large organization, there probably are disgruntled ex-employees 'out there,' and they may have mounted a chat room or newsgroup where you can find out this stuff. Type in the name of the company to MetaCrawler, and see what it turns up. Just remember there are two sides to every story.

But most of the 16,000,000 companies out there don't have such online chat rooms mounted by ex- (or present) employees. All you can find out about the companies online is limited to basic stuff: names, addresses, phone & fax numbers, bottom line, credit rating, and such -- the kind of stuff that you'd want to know before an interview, just to reassure the employer that you care. But more than that is difficult to find online.

Face it: there's only so much the Internet can do. If you're going to go deeper, and find out the information you really want to know, you're going to need to supplement this online research with some offline research -- meaning, you're gonna have to go talk to people, using your contacts, to thoroughly research the companies that interest you. And if you're just too shy or too lazy to do that, then you should use the job interview (when you get it) to explore these questions, as much as you can. Better late than never.

Resources for Those Seeking Self-Employment

<u>Free Agent Nation</u>

```
http://www.fastcompany.com/online/
12/freeagent.html
```

The workplace is changing dramatically. Chief among these changes is the fact that self-employment has become a broader concept in the '90s than it was in another age: it has come to mean any alternative to 'being a lifer' or 'salaryman'/ 'salarywoman' at one company.

Hence the concept now includes not only those who own their own business, but also **free-agents** (independent contractors who work for several clients, plus temps/contract employees who by choice work each day through temporary agencies, plus limited-time-frame workers who work only for a set time, as on a project, then move on to another company, plus consultants, etc.). This is a *lengthy* fascinating article to help you decide if you want to be part of this trend, on the site of a popular magazine (online or off) called *Fast Company*.

Backdoor Jobs

`http://www.backdoorjobs.com/`

For free agents looking for limited-time-frame work (otherwise known as short term jobs) there is this site, by Michael Landes, featuring a sampling from his excellent book, *The Back Door Guide to Short Term Job Adventures.* Basically, he wants you to buy his book (and it's a good book), but there's a lot of useful information and news of opportunities here online even without the book.

Inc. Online's Guide to the Internet

`http://www.inc.com/internet/`

Inc. Magazine sponsors this site, designed for small businesses and those who are self-employed. They have sections on "Getting Started," "Marketing," "Customer Service," etc. with numerous helpful case studies (over 125 of them). You could spend days here.

Entrepreneur Magazine's Small Business Square

`http://www.entrepreneurmag.com/`

They have: lists of Homebased Businesses, Start-Up Ideas, How to Raise Money, Shoestring Startups, Small Business Myths, a Franchise & Business Opportunity Site-Seeing Guide, and a lot more. More days.

Small Business Administration

http://www.sba.gov/starting

Let us not forget the obvious friend of self-employed businesspersons, the U.S. Small Business Administration, which has *a very helpful* site here, loaded with information: FAQs, plus stuff on: Your First Steps, Research, Business Plans, Counseling and Resources, Special Assistance, Business Cards, Shareware Programs, etc., etc.

Yahoo! Small Business Information

http://www.yahoo.com/

Here you can find all kinds of information of interest to the small businessperson, such as stuff about Intellectual Property (copyrights, etc.) or anything else that you're curious about.

Business Resource Center

http://www.greatinfo.com/business_cntr/
bus_res.html

All kinds of resources for the self-employed can be found at The Information Center's site. It leads you to MoneyHunter, a site for seeking investment for your enterprise -- and other interesting places.

iVillage: Work from Home

http://ivillage.com/work/

Self-employment at home is a special case. And this site is superb at marshalling the resources to help.

Newsletter, articles, starter tips, home office basics, expert advice, inspiring stories, message boards, chats -- it's a very impressive site, maintained by iVillage: the women's network.

Freelance Online

```
http://www.FreelanceOnline.com/
wwwboard.html
```

For freelancers in the publishing or advertising fields -- broadcasting, video, editorial, interactive multimedia, writing, art-related, production -- job-hunters can post their bio in this Directory, employers can post opportunities, both can add their two cents to "Open Forum," a bulletin board that has over 2,000 archived messages. A good place to learn a lot. Completely up to date. Maintained by Betsy Keefer.

Resources for Those Seeking Temp Work

The Temp-orary solution

http://www.leggs.com/articles/
9707/temp.C/

An article introducing the concept of choosing to do temporary work, by Annette Lowery. A good primer for beginners, of things you should know before launching into this pursuit.

Temporary Employment: An Overview

http://www.ccsd.ca/insite3.html

The pros & cons of temporary employment. Dated discussion (1995, in Canada) but still interesting.

The Shorter Work Time Action Page

http://www.silcom.com/~rdb/swt/

Discussion, reading, Newsletter, links.

The Contract Employee's Handbook

http://www.cehandbook.com/cehandbook/
htmlpages/ceh_main.html

This is an immensely useful handbook, covering every facet of doing temporary or contract work. The site also has a contract employee's newsletter. It's sponsored by the Professional Association of Contract Employees.

Temporary Relief

```
http://www.disgruntled.com/worksite7.html
http://www.disgruntled.com/
```

Disgruntled: The Business Magazine For People Who Work For A Living, is an interesting site where people can vent. Daniel Levine is one of its regular writers, and in this article, "Temporary Relief," writes a very useful summary of the downside to "life in the temporary trenches," and what resources the Web offers by way of help. Other interesting articles about temp work are also on this site, in "Back Issues."

Temp 24-7

```
http://www.temp24-7.com/
```

A site for, by, and about temporary workers, it strives to be a place where temps can share their stories, gripes, "Temp Tales of Terror," etc. -- and also get advice. They run a contest to name the best and the worst temp agencies, and they plan to include a Temp Help Center and live online chats with temp/career authors.

The Red Guide to Temp Agencies

```
http://www.panix.com/~grvsmth/redguide/
```

Another site -- this one based in New York City -- where temporary workers can share horror stories, warn others not to go near certain agencies, etc. Angus B. Grieve-Smith created this Red Guide. This site, and the one above show what the Web could do for job-hunters, if it were really fulfilling its promise. I wish we had this kind of use of the Web not just in New York City but throughout the whole country, and not only for temp agencies, but for companies, career consultants, everything. Some Usenet groups, of course, do offer similar bulletin boards.

Yahoo!'s List of Temporary Agencies

```
http://www.yahoo.com/Business_and_
Economy/Companies/Employment/Recruiting_
and_Placement/Temporary
```

Yahoo! also posts an extensive list of temporary agencies that have sites on the Internet; you can search by geographical preference.

Resources for Those Interested in Volunteering or Working for Nonprofits

Nonprofit Resources Catalog

```
http://www.clark.net/pub/pwalker/
General_Nonprofit_Resources/
```

So you're interested in working for a nonprofit organization -- either volunteer, part-time, or full-time -- and you're wondering what there is on the Internet about this whole subject? Well, this site has at least 2,897 entries, which should keep you busy more than somewhat. An amazing site, the creation of Phillip A. Walker. He hasn't been able to update since 5/11/97, so some of

148

the info may be (as he says) "stale." But if you keep in mind that new stuff since 5/97 hasn't been catalogued, and some 'old' sites may have vanished, I still think you'll find what is here, extremely useful.

Internet Nonprofit Center

```
http://www.nonprofits.org/
```

Primarily for volunteers (and donors) this site says it has information on more nonprofits than any other site in the world. You'll find information about nonprofits, information by nonprofits -- annual reports, home pages, brochures -- plus chat rooms (called Parlor), bulletin boards, plus a very nice set of links (they call it Heliport) to other sites. They feature prominently the Contact Center Network, now called "Action without Borders" (below).

Action Without Borders

```
http://www.idealist.org/
```

This site has some wonderful lists, categorized by field, state, and country (the directory is worldwide, covering 120 countries). It lists other Nonprofit Directories that are on the Web.

The Argus Clearinghouse: Business & Employment

```
http://www.clearinghouse.net/
cgi-bin/chadmin/viewcat /Business___
Employment/human_resources/non_profit_
organizations?kywd++
```

(That's three "underlines" between "Business" and "Employment" in the URL.) A nice list of sites related to nonprofits: funding, grants, lists of nonprofit organizations, etc. -- with links, of course.

Good Works

`http://www.tripod.com/work/goodworks/search.html`

The search form on this site is superb. You can specify region, state, city, desired compensation and benefits, choose between volunteer, part-time, or full-time, and keyword. It also has a nice dropdown menu called "What's Your Interest?" Alternatively, you can view all nonprofit organizations by title, indexed alphabetically. This site, maintained by Tripod, Inc., is aimed at young adults moving from college into the workplace, but applies to all ages.

Essential Information

`http://www.essential.org/`

Created by Ralph Nader's organization in 1982, Essential Information now has a Web site that lists some actual job listings (on a clickable map of the USA) and links to many Web sites concerned with social change. On this site (under "Good Works") you can also order their book: *Good Works, A Guide to Careers in Social Change* (now in its fifth edition, with information about 1,000 organizations). It's a very useful book, costs $24, and they give you an address you can order it from.

4Work

`http://www.4work.com/`

Here you will find job listings from various business and not-for-profit organizations, internships, youth positions, and volunteer work. Their 'shell' is impressive: a nice search form, and also they have one of those "Search-While-You-Dream" programs. They call it "Job Alert." Great idea! But how much is underneath their 'shell' as I call it, is very difficult to say. For example, I found only 15 job opportunities connected with 'environment' *for the whole country,* when I visited.

Resources on the Internet
for Minorities

VJF Internet Resources for Minorities

```
http://www.hightechcareers.com/
docs/jobsearch.html
```

This site, belonging to *High Technology Careers Magazine,* has Cynthia Chin-Lee's "The Global Village: Resources for Minorities on the Internet." She has a comprehensive list of resources for various minority groups. First rate!

Minorities' Job Bank

```
http://www.minorities-jb.com/
```

An excellent resource for various minorities (African-American, Asian-American, Hispanic-American, Native-American, etc.) with Career Development resources, a job bank, a place to post resumes, etc. The same publisher produces this site, Minorities' Job Bank, and The Black Collegian Online, to which they link.

```
http://black-collegian.com/
```

Saludos Web Career Center

```
http://www.saludos.com/career.html
```

Resources for Hispanics, dealing with careers, education, Internet Resources, etc.

Resources on the Internet for Women

Beatrice's Web Guide

http://www.bguide.com/webguide.careers/

A wonderful site for women, wonderfully designed, with lots of good links. Has "Fab Finds" -- their choice of good sites, dealing with such topics as: Fired?, Entertainment Careers, Job Aptitude and Skills, Salary Info, Starting a Business, Starting a Job-Hunt, Opportunities for Women in Small Business, Working Overseas, etc.

WWWomen

http://www.wwwomen.com/

(Notice: this URL is similar to the URL: http://www.women.com/ for the Women.com network, that includes both Women's Wire, and Beatrice's Web Guide.) Anyway, this site, WWWomen, calls itself "The Premier Search Directory for Women Online." They have all kinds of resources dealing with a woman's whole life: women's resources, women's studies, child support help, resources for single parents, mailing lists, and discussion forums (chat rooms). Under their heading called "Business" they have a huge list of women's associations and women's sites -- the largest in fact that I've seen on the Web.

FeMiNa

```
http://www.femina.com/femina/
BusinessandFinance/
```

Tries to list "female-friendly sites on the Web." Covers a wide variety of sites of interest to women, with links. I found their list impressive.

Women's Wire

```
http://www.womenswire.com/work
```

This site has free advice and referral about childcare, how to set up your home office, keeping your boss in line, job listings, calculators, plus stuff on business travel, eldercare, hot careers, etc. It also has chat rooms and message boards -- on "balance," "career," and "small business." You can sign up for a free newsletter, as well.

Connections

```
http://www.pleiades-net.com/
lists/lists.html
```

A site for women called Pleiades, they maintain two directories to help women get in touch with professional women in various fields. One is called "Women's Directory," and the other is called "Women's Business Directory." In the latter, quite an extensive number of women-owned businesses are listed, with links; however, often these sites -- once you go to them -- look like little more than ads for their services. Still, if you find someone whose work fascinates you, you can always explore the possibility of working with or for them.

Advancing Women

http://www.advancingwomen.com/

This is an international business and career site, dealing with networking, strategy and employment for women who are looking for a new or better job, or ways to advance their career. Features chat rooms, and other resources.

Resources on the Internet for Gays and Lesbians

Yahoo! Company Directories

http://www.yahoo.com/

Yahoo has a most impressive list of gay and lesbian sites, categorized by region; type "gays lesbians" into their search engine, and then when their list comes up, choose the region you wish.

Resources on the Internet for the Elderly

Social Security Administration

http://www.ssa.gov/pubs/10069.html

This site deals with Social Security and retirement. Among other things, this site has useful information about benefits, and advice about how and when to retire.

Resources on the Internet
for People with Disabilities

Employment Resources
for People with Disabilities

```
http://www.disserv.stu.umn.edu/TC/
Grants/COL/listing/disemp/
```

This is a mind-boggling list of employment resources on the Internet for people with disabilities. Someone at the University of Minnesota's Disability Services really did their homework. They have an even larger index at `http://128.101.127.10/index2.html` where, under "In the Spotlight . . .," they list "Disability Related Resources" and "Disability-Specific Web Sites," and -- most interestingly of all -- "Careers Online," which provides a wide variety of services to job-hunters with disabilities, at `http://128.101.127.10/COL/about COL.html`. And I quote, "Anyone who has access to the Internet may reach our services at no fee." Bravo.

The Job Accommodation Network: The ADA

```
http://janweb.icdi.wvu.edu/kinder/
```

This site has a tremendous amount of useful information about disabilities, starting with the Americans with Disabilities Act. Created by Duncan C. Kinder.

Click on "Links to Related Sites," and they give you a good list of other Internet Disability Sites, as well as sites dealing with particular diseases and other disabilities.

Click on "Job Accommodation Network," and you will

be taken to a variety of resources. They provide, by telephone, individualized searches for workplace accommodations, based on the job's functional requirements, the functional limitations of the individual, and other pertinent information.

WORKink

http://www.workink.com/

A Canadian site for people with disabilities, that gives you access to a live counselor (believe it or not) -- either by signing up in advance, or by "dropping in" between 10 and 11 a.m. EST. It also has helpful resources for people with disabilities.

Research Sites: Standard Reference Works

I mean things like: *dictionaries, encyclopedias, access to Libraries on the Internet,* and the like.

Merriam Webster

http://www.m-w.com/netdict.htm

This site has both a dictionary and a thesaurus -- for help while writing your resume, thank-you letter, or whatever.

OneLook Dictionaries

http://www.onelook.com/

If Merriam Webster turns up nothing, this is your lifeboat: they have indexed at least 376 dictionaries, with over 1,960,863 words in them. Tell them what word you want defined, or spelled, or pronounced, and they will tell you what online dictionary or dictionaries have your word. They'll offer you a link to said dictionary's page(s). Click, you're there.

Research-It!

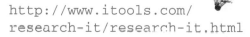

```
http://www.itools.com/
research-it/research-it.html
```

This site has links to an incredible number of standard research tools: searchable Dictionaries (English, Computing, Rhyming, Pronouncing); a searchable Thesaurus; Translators (will translate to or from any of more than 22 languages); a Language Identifier; an Acronym dictionary; plus research tools dealing with People, Religion, Quotations, Maps, Telephone Directories, CIA Factbook, Currency Converters, Discussion Groups on the Internet, etc., etc. A great site!

Internet Public Library Reference Center

```
http://www.ipl.org/ref/
```

Intended to be an online reference library for the Internet, this site has links to online general reference works, plus specialized reference works dealing with business and economics, associations, social sciences, arts & humanities, health & medical sciences, law, government & political sciences. (Cute home page for the

Reference Center.) It would be difficult to think of any online reference work that isn't linked to, from this site. An amazing contribution to the Internet.

Online reference works

`http://www.cs.cmu.edu/references.html`

This list supplements and in some instances duplicates the IPL (above) -- but it has a good compendium of online standard reference works: dictionaries (English and foreign), thesauri, quotations, encyclopedias, internet resources, place-oriented references, almanacs, and general reference.

The Online Books Page

`http://www.cs.cmu.edu/books.html`

Well, *of course* every book ever written is *not* online -- only those that are 'beyond copyright.' But 7,000+ books or articles are online; and you can search them here, all at once, by author, title, or subject (useful if you're away from home with your laptop and you're *desperate* to read something, even if it's on a computer screen). A helpful site, maintained by John Mark Ockerbloom.

If You Want Further Education

Today, This Very Day (or Night)

If the night is still young after you've found what you were researching, then -- by all means -- have fun on the Internet. A job-hunt should have its periods of relaxation, as long as in between those periods there are also periods of good hard, get-out-of-the-house, pavement-pounding, work. See what you can learn that has nothing to do with your job-hunt!

Learn2.com, the ability utility

http://www.learn2.com/

This is a reference site for your continuing education on a variety of abilities or skills: communication skills, financial skills, childcare skills, on-the-job skills, and a variety of other life themes, such as food, health, hobbies, sports, etc. It has "2torials" (*cute*) on how to avoid repetitive stress, how to block out sounds in a room, how to cope with insomnia, how to repair a scratched CD, how to get a clean comfortable shave, how to whistle, how to make a perfect pot of tea, how to deal with your laundry, how to find and hire a nanny, etc. New material is posted endlessly. *Yahoo! Internet Life* calls it "The #1 most incredibly useful site on the Web."

Another way to learn is to do random learning by using Yahoo!'s random generator (http://random.yahoo.com/bin/ryl) *repeatedly*. It will take you places you wouldn't choose on your own, and thus you'll learn all about different sites (and subjects) on the Internet.

Short Term, By Books or Newsletters

If on the Internet you can't find what you're looking for, you might want to see if there is a book that could tell you what you want to know. You can at least search for it, online, by subject; then, once you have a title in mind, go to your public library to check it out. Or, if it's inexpensive and you can afford it, you can also order it online:

amazon.com

```
http://www.amazon.com/
```

bookworm

```
http://www.ads-links.com/
bookworm/index.html
```

Amazon.com is the place where I would start with my book research. If you want more places to search or to order from, Bookworm has a complete catalog of all the bookstores that are online, with links.

The Newsletter Library

http:www.newsletter-library.com/

If there's some hobby, interest, or subject you want to know more about, chances are there's a newsletter in that field that you can get your hands on. 11,000 of them are available, from this site. "11,000 free newsletters," they say; well, not exactly. It's 11,000 free *samples* of newsletters, that you can order, so as to help you decide whether or not ultimately to subscribe.

Long Term, with Colleges, Universities, etc.

The Argus Clearinghouse: Education

http://www.clearinghouse.net/cgi-bin/ chadmin/viewcat /Education?kywd++

This contains a list of guides (with links) on topics pertaining to where to get additional skills and education that you want to obtain -- by systematic instruction, schooling, training, or guidance.

Colleges & Careers Center

http://www.usnews.com/usnews/edu/home.htm

U.S. News' rankings of 1,300 colleges. Tips on how to "Find Your Ideal School," tips on finding the best grad schools (Law, Medicine, Engineering, Education and Business), tips on financial aid (with worksheets), etc. It also has forums (called the "Answer Zone") where you can post your questions on Getting into College, Beyond College, and Financial Aid.

5.

Sites Where You Can Make Contacts

Subjects

in This Section on Contacts

The Fairy Godmother Report on Contact Sites

What You'd Hope to Find

What You Actually Get   How Effective

Words to Remember

Sites for Making Contacts: **If You Know Who**

(or Whom) You Want to Reach

If You Don't Know Who (or Whom) You Want to Reach

Chat Rooms   Message Boards or Newsgroups

Mailing Lists   Gopher Sites

Sites

in this section on Contacts, with Descriptions and Links

the pagesite.com   555-1212.com

Four11   Switchboard   WhoWhere?

Europages   Email Address Finding Tools

ZipFind   Synapse Internet

Contact Center Network
Publicly Accessible Mailing Lists
Liszt   CareerMagazine   CareerMosaic   dejanews
BranchOut

In its essence all job-hunting is a search not only for information, but also for people -- that is, for human links between you and information, between you and a prospective employer, or if you choose self-employment, between you and prospective clients. These human links are called 'contacts.'

The
Fairy Godmother Report:
Sites Where You Can Make Contacts

WHAT YOU'D HOPE TO FIND: You'd hope that the Internet would turn out to be your fairy godmother: that on the Internet you could search for (and find) contacts who could help you with your job-hunt; and find them faster and more reliably than you ever could in real life. You'd hope for contacts who could serve two purposes: be able to tell you information you couldn't find out any other way; and help get you in to a particular place where you wanted to work.

WHAT YOU ACTUALLY GET: Just what you'd hope for. Finding contacts is one of those tasks at which the Internet absolutely excels. On the Internet, you can find someone in another geographical place, even another country, someone in another company, someone in another field, someone with the same interest as yours, someone who's an expert in a field you don't know anything about, etc., etc. -- *and* you can find them faster than a speeding bullet. So far as finding contacts and making contact is concerned, the Internet *is* your fairy godmother.

HOW EFFECTIVE: My personal estimate of the effectiveness of this use of the Internet, in getting a job: *ho boy* -- it's difficult to estimate because if it's *information* you basically want from them, everything depends on how crucial that information is (or is not) to your job-hunt. On the other hand, if you want them to kick open doors for you at the organization(s) of your choice, well, *that* effectiveness rate I estimate at 20 percent. That is: out of every 100 people who find contacts on the Internet, 20 of them will be able to use them to actually find a job. I think 80 will not. Though even in the latter case their online contacts may give them very useful information and suggestions prior to the hiring interview.

WORDS YOU MAY HAVE CAUSE TO REMEMBER: In any job-hunting that is worthy of the name, contacts are often the secret of the game. It takes a village to help you find a job; and, these days, part of that village is found on the Internet.

Sites for Making Contacts

If You Know Who (or Whom) You Want To Reach:

The Internet can help you make contact with them instantly, by using e-mail. No more waiting five days for surface mail to get there, and then wondering if it ever did.

Here are sites to help you locate the person you're trying to get in touch with:

the pagesite.com

http://www.thepagesite.com/findcp.htm

Links to an impressive list of at least 35 different kinds of phone directories, to help you search for area codes, e-mail addresses, phone numbers, etc. It also has interest groups, genealogy resources, a phone number speller (!), etc.

555-1212.com

http://www.555-1212.com/

This site says it will look up area codes, telephone numbers including a reverse directory (number --> name), e-mail addresses, and Web sites for you. I tested it, of course, with individual names or phone numbers of persons I already knew, and unfortunately quite often 555-1212.com could not find that individual in its databases. When it did find a match, it gave the wrong town and zipcode, and the wrong e-mail addresses in several

cases. In light of all this, I quote this interesting little factoid they have on their site (the bold emphasis is theirs):

"There are quite a few United States White Pages telephone directories available on the Internet. **None of the directories that we're aware of gets their information direct from any of the major telephone companies.** Instead, they all utilize data gathered by just three different information vendors *(Database America, Metromail, and ProCD)* . . . **Don't waste your time.** If you don't find the person's telephone number you're looking for from one of the directories . . . then chances are you probably won't find it listed in any telephone directory on the Internet. Good luck!" (Some telephone sites also draw on the database of *infoUSA Inc.*)

Now, the following famous sites are subject to the same problems as 555-1212.com, but in case you want to try *everything* to find someone, here they are.

Four11

http://www.Four11.com/

Metromail is the database provider here. It's subject to the same problems as 555-1212.com.

Switchboard

http://www.switchboard.com/

infoUSA Inc. is the database provider here, though apparently the site was started by Database America. It's subject to the same problems as 555-1212.com.

WhoWhere?

http://www.whowhere.com/

I like this site, even though I often 'strike out' when using it to look up somebody. But it has a variety of services that I appreciate: e-mail lookup, advanced community searches by location, school, personal interests, etc. for those who have registered with WhoWhere; a directory of one million personal home pages on the Web; EDGAR filings (for Security Exchange Commission files on specified public corporations); links to over 50 different international phone directories, and more. They can display in English, Japanese, French or Spanish.

Europages, The European Business Directory

http://www.europages.com/

For those looking for contacts in Europe, this site has 500,000 company names (no links) and snail-mail addresses from over 25 European countries, with links to each country's phone book (their Yellow Pages). You can search by country, subject, company name, etc. Once you've found a company in the Yellow Pages, in the subject area that interests you, you are left to explore who to get in touch with, there.

Email Address-Finding Tools

http://twod.med.harvard.edu/labgc/
roth/Emailsearch.html

Here are enough tools that should help you find the email address of almost *anyone*. Of course, as with all Internet tools, you still can strike out.

ZipFind

`http://link-usa.com/zipcode/`

If you want to find the ZIP codes for a particular city, this is the site to come to. In addition to looking up the city of your choice, it will also find all zip codes within a given radius, plus tell you the distance between two different zip codes.

My overall advice, if you're looking for a specific person by name, as a potential contact: be *sure* to use all of these programs. Sometimes two of them will miss, but the third will tell you exactly what you want to know.

You will want to remember, of course, that anyone you contact on the Internet should be approached -- as in *real* life -- respectfully, politely, courteously, with keen awareness on your part that this is a very busy person, who may or may not be able to respond. If they do give you any help, e-mail thank-you notes should *always* be sent to them, *promptly* (within three days) for the help they gave you.

If You Don't Know Who (or Whom)
You Want To Reach:

So, you don't know anybody. Never fear. The number of contacts you can make online is absolutely mind-boggling. Any faraway place that interests you, you'll likely find a contact online. Any question you need an answer to, you'll likely find someone online who knows the answer. Any organization where you need to know how to meet 'the-person-who-has-the-power-to-hire,' you'll likely find someone online who knows somebody who . . .

And how do you find these people? Well, you can locate them by interest or speciality, or company, or geography, or any other matching word you can think of; and you can do that on the following *kinds* of sites *(skip this section if you already know all this):*

- **Chat Rooms** (these are places where you 'meet with' other people, online, at the same time, and have a chat with each other on your computer screen, using your keyboard. It's like watching the dialogue from a play script unfold line by line on your screen. Chat rooms are found on commercial services such as *America Online,* and on Web services such as *Yahoo!*'s 'Chat & Boards') In choosing which ones to sign on to, you can search by subject, matching word, etc.
- **Message Boards or Newsgroups** (a 'newsgroup' is like a discussion group devoted to some field of interest, where the members arrive at different times, and leave their message on an electronic bulletin board which other members of the group can come later to read, and reply to.) Message Boards are found on the Web at such sites as *Yahoo!*'s Chat & Boards. Newsgroups or discussion groups are located on a part of the Internet called 'Usenet,' and are accessible through your Web browser *(so long as your Internet Service Provider gives you Usenet access).* In choosing which discussion group(s) to sign up for, you can search by subject, matching word, etc. *Note: some job-hunters shy away from UseNet discussion groups, because junk e-mail firms often crawl the UseNet, picking up ("harvesting" is what it's called) your e-mail address therefrom, and then*

bombarding you with junk mail ("spam"). But see dejanews below, which offers protection against this.

- **Mailing Lists** (these are discussion groups similar to Message Boards or newsgroups, except that every message from every member in the group is automatically sent to your e-mail address. You don't have to go to a bulletin board site to get the messages -- the messages come to you.) In choosing which ones to sign up for, you can search by subject, matching word, etc.

- **Gopher Sites** ("gopher" is a menu-driven system of getting information; it pre-dates the Web, but its sites are accessible through your Web browser). It is searchable by subject, matching word, etc.

And now, here are the ways of searching such sites:

Message Boards, Newsgroups and Mailing Lists

Finding newsgroups or mailing lists

`http://www.synapse.net/~radio/finding.htm`

This site here, run by Synapse Internet, has a good list of such places, and how to find them.

Idealist–Directory

`http://www.idealist.org/`

This excellent site lists over 15,000 organizations, publications, nonprofits, and community organizational interests. You can browse around the world, by country, or by keyword. Great site!

Publicly Accessible Mailing Lists

`http://www.neosoft.com/internet/paml/`

Finding contacts by interest field can also be done on this site, maintained by NeoSoft™. It has a wonderful list that can be accessed by subject, name, or title.

Liszt, The Mailing List Directory

`http://www.Liszt.com`

Their "spider" goes out each week to search for all the major USENET Newsgroups and all Mailing Lists anywhere in the world. Last I looked, it had over 90,000 mailing lists in its directory.

CareerMagazine

`http://www.careermag.com/using.html`

This is for job contacts. Every day CareerMagazine downloads and indexes all the job listings "from all the major Internet jobs newsgroups," and then offers the ability to search these jobs by keyword, location, skills, and title. You can designate "Most relevant jobs first," or "Most recent jobs first." Be forewarned, however, that in spite of all these newsgroups' postings and this nice interface, you can still 'strike out.'

CareerMosaic

`http://www.careermosaic.com/cm/cm36.html`

This is also for job contacts. This famous site gathers over 60,000 job listings daily from over 80 USENET newsgroups (which it lists, by name). You can search them all at once, with specific parameters; their index is rebuilt every 24 hours "on a rolling basis;" and their postings are purged every seven days.

dejanews

```
http://www.dejanews.com/categories/
jobs.shtml
```

Has messages from over 60,000+ Newsgroups, going back for two years. It lists all kinds of interest groups, by topic. If it's job listings you're looking for, just type in your query, like: jobs AND Bay Area and it will give you the actual job listings that match, in reverse order (most recent, first). On that part of their site called "My Deja News" they filter out commercial messages in their discussion forums, "so you get virtually spam-free reading!" Also, in partnership with WhoWhere? Inc., they offer each user a free e-mail service that is (hopefully) 'spam-free' as well.

BranchOut

```
http://www.BranchOut.com/Tourstats.htm
```

This is an informal experiment, to see if alumni from particular colleges can contact one another and help one another *online*. BranchOut presently has at least 45 colleges or universities as pilot projects -- principally Ivy League or Jesuit Educational Institutions -- with more to come; and the signed-up alumni (when last I looked) represented 98 industries (principally computer, financial, consulting, law, and education); 101 job functions (principally marketing manager, consultant, entrepreneur-owner, engineer, and general manager); 42 countries (though the U.S. represents 85% of the database); and 715 cities (N.Y., Boston, San Francisco, Philadelphia, and Washington, D.C. are the most represented). *It will be interesting to see where this experiment goes; it has great potential -- either to be the biggest 'snob network' on the Internet, or an opening up of alumni lists worldwide.*

If You 'Strike Out' on the Internet and Can't Find A Job

Well, that is the end of our guide to Job-hunting on the Internet. If all the resume postings and the job listings you search pay off for you, and you get the job you most desire, *great!* But, if it doesn't, please don't take it personally.

If you're job-hunting on the Internet, and nothing turns up for you, that's because the job posting sites and the resume posting sites on the Internet just present us with the old Neanderthal job-hunting system our country loves and knows so well, albeit in a new dress. That system didn't work very well before the Internet, and it doesn't work very well now.

Don't let anyone tell you "It's you, who are the problem." No, no, dear friend. It's our Neanderthal job-hunting system that's the problem. That system doesn't pay off for a large proportion of those who come on to the Internet with hopes high. Let me show you what I mean:

Reports from The Field:
The Experience of Actual job-hunters
Concerning Their Resume (and Job Listings)
On The Internet This Past Year Or So

Jobhunter #1. *I have not had any positive reaction to any of my listings of my resume online. The one exception was a head-hunter who asked for my resume. You will get a lot of offers from strange companies or people looking for things that I would describe as pyramid schemes.*

Jobhunter #2. It was a waste of my time . . . not a single reply!

Jobhunter #3. *I haven't gotten any responses online. My impression is that if you're not in the computer field, you can pretty much forget finding work online.*

Jobhunter #4. I found the Internet to be very limited, even for computer employment (which is what I do). Even the 'Entry-Level' newsgroup is full of jobs requiring previous experience. Most of the employer listings seem to be looking for another Albert Einstein with just as many years of experience.

Jobhunter #5. *I didn't actually get my job from the Net, though I made a pass at it. But in the end, I probably reverted to old habits rather than pursuing the job search on the Net the way I said I would. At the same time, the Net definitely played a part in my job-hunt, as I pursued many of my contacts via*

e-mail -- much better than making 'cold' telephone calls, once I'd gotten an e-mail address for a contact in a company (for some reason, a much easier thing than getting direct phone numbers). If I had it to do over again, I would probably do more to take advantage of the Net . . .

Jobhunter #6. I found seeking work online was worth-while, but I'm in computer programming. After watching the listings for a few weeks, I saw a posting in mid-December which I answered with an e-mailed cover letter and resume. I heard back within a few hours, indicating they would be in touch when they scheduled interviews. While waiting to hear back, I saw another posting for which I considered myself qualified (Note: only two listings that fitted me at all, in four weeks). I answered this one, but never heard back. However, the first one did call me back four weeks later, to set up an appointment, and they offered me the job two weeks after that. I started three weeks after that. But notice how long this process took. While you connect quickly on the Internet, the employment process still moves at a snail's pace 'out there.' You'll need patience. Big time patience.

Jobhunter #7. *I feel that online job lists should be viewed with the same healthy skepticism that we offer to want ads. That is, there are many scams, there are comparatively few jobs outside high tech, the government, and academe, and the qualifications sought are either high or highly specialized. Thus, one should not spend any greater time online than he or she would spend looking at the want ads. There is more hype than substance for the so-called average job seeker.*

In sum, I agree with Margaret F. Dikel (formerly Margaret Riley), everybody's favorite expert on electronic job-hunting, whose words I quoted elsewhere in this Guide: "The Internet is merely an added dimension to the traditional job search, and it is not necessarily an easy dimension to add."

But if you're determined to try it, my advice is: budget only a certain amount of your total job-hunting time to *the Internet part of your job-search* (I'd say 15% of your time, *max*). Keep tabs on yourself, and if after two weeks you discover that the Internet is *all* you are doing with your life, disconnect, give your modem to a friend, and go back to job-hunting the *old way:* the way people job-hunted before the computer was ever discovered.

But in either case, *follow the creative method of job-hunting,* puh-leaze.

That method has eight simple rules:

   I. Know your best and most enjoyable transferable skills.

  II. Know what kind of work you want to do, what field you would most enjoy working in.

 III. Talk to people who are doing the work you want to do, in that field. Find out how they like the work, how they found their job.

 IV. Do some research, then, in your chosen geographical area on those organizations which interest you, to find what they do and what kinds of problems/challenges they or their industry are wrestling with.

  V. Then identify and seek out the person who actually has the power to hire you at each organization, for the job you want; use your personal contacts -- everyone you know -- to get in to see him or her.

VI.   Show this person with the power to hire you how you can help them with their problems/needs/challenges; and how you would stand out as 'one employee in a hundred.'

VII. Don't take turndown or rejection personally. Remember, there are two kinds of employers out there: those who will be bothered by your handicaps -- age, background, inexperience, or whatever they are -- and those who won't be, and will hire you, so long as you can do the job. If you get rejected by the first kind of employer, keep persevering, until you find the second.

VIII. In all of this, cut no corners, take no shortcuts.

If you need further help with this method, rather than just with online job-hunting, go read the current edition of *What Color Is Your Parachute?* It's in all the bookstores. A new, updated edition comes out each year, reaching the bookstores (usually) between October 15th and November 20th. See page 194.

**"There are tons of jobs out there
that the Web knows nothing about!"**

Appendix

A Beginner's Primer:
The Internet

THE HISTORY

If you're a beginner with the Internet, and you want to understand it, it might be helpful to look at a little history first.

We may think of the last three decades, *computer-wise*, in broad brush strokes such as these:

The '70s may be thought of as largely The Era Of The **Mainframe** Computer. It was a huge thing, that could fill a whole room. Hooked up to it, were *terminals*, smaller machines that were used to run programs on the mainframe. (The mainframe acted as what would later be called a *server* -- defined as anything that provides services to another computer.)

With the coming of the '80s we moved into a new era: The Era Of The **Desktop** Computer. Manufacturers were able to put on each person's desk a computer that was self-contained with its own data-storage system -- ultimately, hard disk(s). These were computers requiring connection to nothing else, and, by the late '80s, nearly the equal of some of the old mainframes, in terms of computing power and speed.

With the coming of the '90s we moved into still another era: which may be thought of, loosely, as The **Union** Of Mainframe And Desktop. *A kind-of Mainframe* has returned, not as a replacement for the desktop computer, but as an adjunct to it. What is different from the '70s is that this *kind-of Mainframe* is not constructed as one big computer filling a huge room, but as a number of networks of computer sites around the world deciding to voluntarily link up with each other -- desktop and mainframe alike -- so that *together* they act *as if* they were a *kind-of humongous Mainframe.* And the name of this *Mainframe-like thing* is The Internet, 'cause it's a series of links *between* (hence: *Inter-*) a whole *network of networks* (hence: *-Net*) of computers around the world.

When, therefore, you connect to the Internet today you are seeking out this thing we might call (by way of *very very* loose metaphor) *The World's Largest Mainframe,* and linking it with your desktop computer -- whereupon you too become *part of the Internet* -- which has one part in Michigan, one part in Sweden, one part in Worcester, one part in Australia, one part in Berkeley, and so on and so forth.

But in spite of the scatteredness of its parts, what is ingenious about the thing is that it performs essentially as though it were one (though with unpredictable flaws).

THE BIRTH OF 'THE BLUES'

I characterized the Internet, above, as a creature of the '90s. Actually, it existed for a couple of decades before that. It just never became really popular with *the masses,* until the '90s. It is easy to explain why.

First proposed in the '60s by RAND Corporation, MIT and UCLA, the Internet actually began in 1969 as part of the Pentagon's Advanced Research Projects. Their concern was to ensure that information could be sent around the world in peacetime or wartime, even if particular cities -- hence computer sites -- were destroyed (*this is why the Internet breaks down a message into electronic 'packets,' then has those packets take random routes to their destination, where they are then reassembled*).

The Pentagon's concerns aside, the Internet quickly got adopted as a kind of high-speed electronic post office, and in the 1980's expanded to include the National Science Foundation's supercomputer sites, as well as university, library and research centers' sites.

Nonetheless, it remained largely the domain of a kind of 'computer aristocracy': defense people, computer programmers, and academic types. It didn't attract a wider audience for a number of reasons. For one thing, there were several different *models of data*, hence *protocols* or *rules*, that each Internet *host* could adopt. These protocols had such names as *telnet, ftp, gopher, usenet, listserv, e-mail,* and the like, and each node or host computer on the Internet could decide what model or protocol it wished to adopt for its site.

What these protocols had in common was that their data appeared on your computer screen as essentially *text, text, text* -- no color, no pictures, no pizazz, no nothin'. *(You* could *download pictures to your own computer, but they were binary files which had been* uuencoded, *and basically looked like a mess of gibberish -- until once they were downloaded to your desktop computer, you* uudecoded *them, back into their original binary code. Then, and only then, a picture would slowly appear on your desktop. It all was and is a very big royal pain.)*

And that was the state of the Internet when, finally, along came *the World Wide Web.* At last: Lights! Camera! Action! Text in colors: yellows, reds, and blues!

THE WORLD WIDE WEB (W³)

In 1990, Tim Berners-Lee, at CERN, the Ruropean Particle Physics Laboratory in Geneva, Switzerland, conceived the idea of applying an already existent technology called *hypertext* to networked computers. Thus was born (a year later) a new Internet protocol, destined to be called *the World Wide Web.*

Hypertext was used by Tim to magically transport you to a different computer site, different file, etc., *among networked computers* anywhere on the Internet, anywhere in the world -- when you mouse-clicked on a designated word, series of words, graphic, or other *hyperlinks* on your screen.

This enabled users of the Web to leap from one Internet site to another, like a gazelle. In fact, at a time of day when the Web isn't overloaded with traffic, this leaping can be as fast as 1–5 seconds, from site to site. *(On slow days, of course, it can take much longer, and sometimes a site won't even come up on your computer, because too many people are trying to contact it at the same time -- and it is overloaded.)*

In a sense, this wasn't new; the protocol called *gopher* already enabled you to leap around this quickly in *gopherspace* on the Internet. But on the Web, married to this ability *to leap* was the ability *to display pictures, graphics, charts, visuals, and sound,* on your computer monitor. Even the old *text, text, text* could be all gussied up, in colors, so that it looked *pretty.*

In terms of the *state of the art* of the Internet, this was like going from radio to color television, in the blink of an eye. You, the idle consumer, could now get on the Internet, and instead of looking at text, text, text, you could see some really interesting graphics and color and visuals on your desktop computer screen. With the World Wide Web, the Internet had acquired a new face, *inter-face,* that is, and new makeup. It had color. It had pictures. It looked *wonderful.*

Moreover, you could create your own *'Web site'* and *'Web page,'* if you wished, and on that page *(or pages)* display whatever you wanted to. It was, and is, democracy in action.

With the invention of *the Web* interface, the Internet suddenly became *really* interesting to average, everyday people. People perked up. The Internet started attracting the masses, by the millions. Even if you didn't have access to a computer at work, a desktop computer at home could give you access to the Internet with just a *modem* (installed or added to your computer), *a telephone line* running from the phone company's wall plug to your modem, and some *Internet Service Provider* -- in some cases your phone company, who, for a fee, would connect you to the Internet.

YOUR EXPERIENCE WITH THE INTERNET

And when you have all this equipment up and running, what then? Well, I would say that your feelings about the Internet will largely depend on how many experiences you have that are described (next page) in the left-hand column, vs. how many experiences you have that are described in the right-hand column there:

HAPPY EXPERIENCES	UNHAPPY EXPERIENCES
The computer equipment necessary for going "online" is within your budget, and relatively inexpensive.	The computer equipment necessary for going "online" is more than your budget can stand (particularly if you're unemployed as you read this).
The modem is already installed inside your computer, or else connecting it to your computer is 'a piece of cake.'	Connecting the modem to the computer is a process so difficult it drives you to tears.
Getting an online provider who has a local access phone number is easy. It's your telephone company, or someone else who makes it easy.	Finding a decent online provider where you live, with a local access phone number, is extremely difficult.
Hooking up via the online provider is easy, because they give you all the information you need in order to be able to do it easily, and they stand by with telephone trouble-shooting. Additionally, you have friends who have the same kind of computer you do, are already on the Internet, and are anxious to guide and help you all the way.	Hooking up via the online provider is difficult, because they give you little or none of the information you need in order to be able to do it correctly, and their technicians are unavailable or ignorant of your system. To compound the difficulties, you have no friends who are already on the Internet. Hence, you are basically working blind here, and the temptation to throw the whole thing out the window gets stronger by the minute.
The online provider is inexpensive.	Charges mount by the minute, while you are online to the Web.
You can usually dial right into the Web, without any trouble, through your online provider; their modem, their server's performance, and their Internet connections are all fast.	You get the equivalent of constant busy signals from your online provider many times when you try to get on the Internet; their equipment is often overloaded or 'down.' (AOL comes to mind.)

HAPPY EXPERIENCES	UNHAPPY EXPERIENCES
You have a fast computer plus a fast modem which runs at 56K bps, or an ISDN or T1 line, or (wonder of wonders) a cable-modem running at 50 to 100 times the speed of a 28.8 K modem -- hence images and Web pages load lightning fast.	Your computer is slow, and/or you have a modem which runs at 28.8K bps or less, hence information loads *painfully* slowly.
Once you are on the Web, you zoom. Your favorite 'search engine' appears on the screen almost immediately, you choose a site and ask your browser to take you there, and you are there almost immediately.	Sometimes "connections are maddeningly slow, and systems often impenetrable" (*Neil Winton, Reuters*). Once you are connected to the Web through your browser and your favorite 'search engine,' you ask it to take you to the site you want, but you run into a traffic jam. Or you are rejected with some such message as: "The server may not be accepting connections or may be busy. Try again later." You're going to have to come back later (try midnight) before you can get in.
You can always find the Web page that you are seeking.	You can't find a Web page that you know is out there. You get a message like: "404 Not Found -- file doesn't exist," or "This server has no DNS." But you *know* it's out there, somewhere.
The Web page you want to see comes up on your screen almost immediately.	It takes too long to download and view the Web pages you want.
When you reach a particular site, you discover it was 'exactly as advertised,' and you find just what you want.	When you reach a particular site, you discover *they lied.* e.g., they claim 15,000 employers are listing their vacancies on that site, but at the time you call you find only 22. Or they claim they have *nationwide job listings,* but you discover *that* totals only 50 -- one for each state. And so forth. And so on.

HOW IT ALL WORKS: URLs

And how should it work, once you're 'on the Internet?' Well, on your screen should be your 'browser' -- Netscape Navigator, or Microsoft Internet Explorer, in all likelihood. If there's some site you want to go to -- you saw it mentioned somewhere, and you know **the electronic address** of that site, sometimes called its "**Location**" or "**URL**" *which stands* for *Uniform Resource Locator* -- all you have to do is type the URL *(carefully)* into the window toward the top of your browser, (on Netscape Navigator the little strip window is called "Netsite") hit the return key on your computer, and -- magically -- your browser will take you to that site.

The URL leads directly to the site wherever it is in the world, and to the file you seek; this is the reason every company or venture is putting their 'web address' (URL) at the bottom of their newspaper or magazine ad -- if they have a page on the Web. You probably will see it in shorthand like:

```
www.metacrawler.com
```

You, however, must type in the **full** URL, which usually begins with http://:

```
http://www.metacrawler.com/
```

SEARCH ENGINES AND DIRECTORIES

URLs are *tres* important. But even if you were to learn the URLs of, say, all the famous employment sites on the Internet, such as CareerMosaic, the Monster Board, America's Job Bank, etc., still you could not possibly keep up with what's on the Internet in general, and the World Wide Web in particular.

You're dead on the Internet unless they give us a table of contents or an index.

Fortunately for you and me, people have come up with an index to the Internet -- actually, a number of *indices*. As an overall category they are loosely called 'Search Engines.' They have weird names, like: *Yahoo!, Excite, InfoSeek, AltaVista, HotBot, MetaCrawler*, and so forth. But, weird names aside, once you are on the Internet, you are going to become very familiar with them, because without them, you'll *never* make your way around the Internet.

How do you find a search engine? Usually, your 'browser' (like Netscape Navigator or Microsoft Internet Explorer) begins by displaying a 'search page' for you. Alternatively, you can choose one you like and make it your 'home page' (see your browser's manual for directions on how to do this). My personal favorite is MetaCrawler (its URL is the one I just mentioned, above).

Whichever search engine you use, it usually has a little box with the word "Search" or "Go" beside it. To conduct a search, you type within that little white box some keyword or words indicating what you'd like to find, and then you mouse-click on the *Search* button next to it.

What kind of keywords do you type in? Well, you might type in words such as "Jobs AND Seattle," if that were your interest. Or "Career advice," or "Companies," "Microsoft," "Weather," "social careers," or whatever. Anything about which you're looking for more information.

The engine will then search with lightning speed (we hope) through its entire index of the Internet *(the very bottom of your browser's screen tells you what it's doing)* after which it will give you a list, on screen, of whatever it's found that even *vaguely* matches what you asked for.

If you see something you like, on that list -- you may not -- you mouse-click on the file name or URL, and magically the Web transports you to the site on the Internet that has that file, no matter where in the world it may be physically located. Voila! The file opens up, and your browser displays it on your computer. *Unless, of course, you've run into a traffic jam on the information superhighway -- in which case, you'll have to come back, a few minutes or hours from now.*

> *The things that are most critical for you to understand, and be at home with on the Web, are not the URLs of famous employment sites, but the search engines. It's the only way you are going to keep up with what's on the Internet in general, and the World Wide Web in particular.*

Mastering the Internet

If you want to know more about the Internet and you know enough to at least get on the Internet, here are the URLs you may want to go to:

Tutorials
Guides and Tutorials

```
http://www.alabanza.com/kabacoff/
Inter-Links/guides.html
```

Here you have extended guides to the Internet and various subjects under that general heading.

Words

PC Webopaedia

http://www.pcwebopedia.com/

Can't keep "browser" straight, from "search engine"? Here is the site for you.

It's an online dictionary of the vocabulary of the Internet. Give them a word you're stumped by (like "emoticon"), and they'll tell you what it means, along with "Related Terms" and "Related Categories."

The Web

Navigating the World Wide Web

http://www.imagescape.com/helpweb/www/www.html

This site has helpful tutorials on such subjects as "An Overview of the World Wide Web," "Finding Something on the Web," "A Consumer's Guide to Search Engines," "Netscape Hints," "Multimedia on the Web," and "Bookmarks."

Search Engines

Search Engine Watch

http://searchenginewatch.internet.com/

This site has everything you could possibly want to know about search engines. There's a guide for first time visitors. There's "Search Engine Status Report," reviews and comparisons of various search engines, tutorials on how to use them, history of the major engines, and search engines in the news.

Browsers

<u>Browserwatch</u>

http://www.browserwatch.com

This site has everything you could possibly want to know about browsers.

BOOKS

If you want more help before going online, then a book is your ticket. You can go to your local library or bookstore and get one or two books on the following booklist:

The Guide to Internet Job Searching by Margaret F. Riley, Frances Roehm, and the late Steve Oserman (Foreword by Tom Jackson). VGM Career Horizons, a division of NTC Publishing Group, Lincolnwood, Illinois, 1998 (Second Edition). *An extraordinary work. If you can buy or read only one book, I suggest that this be it. The authors plan to update it, regularly, though sadly Steve died this year (1998).*

As I mentioned earlier, the online companion to their book is called the Riley Guide, and it can be found at the URL:
http://www.dbm.com/jobguide/

Also useful:

CAREERXROADS: career (cross) roads, by Gerry Crispin & Mark Mehler. MNC Group, Kendall Park, NJ, 1998. Its subtitle says it all: "The 1998 Directory to the 500 Best Job, Resume and Career Management Sites on the World Wide Web, with 500 reviews of the WWW's best sites for finding jobs and resumes -- with free updates!"

How to Get Your Dream Job Using the Web, by Shannon Karl and Arthur Karl. The Coriolanus Group, 1997. Contains a CD-ROM.

Be Your Own Headhunter Online, by Pam Dixon & Sylvia Tiersten. Random House, 1995.

Using the Internet in Your Job Search, by Fred E. Jandt & Mary B. Nemnich. JIST Works, Inc., 1995.

Finding A Job On The Internet, by Alfred and Emily Glossbrenner. McGraw-Hill, 1995.

The Online Job Search, by James C. Gonyea (Foreword by Tom Jackson). McGraw-Hill, 1995.

Hook Up, Get Hired! The Internet Job Search Revolution, by Joyce Lain Kennedy. John Wiley & Sons, Inc., 1995. Joyce, a famous syndicated columnist who was very kind to me in the early days of Parachute, became a pioneer and an acknowledged leader on the subject of electronic job-hunting, by virtue of this book and two earlier ones on the same subject, namely:

The Electronic Job Search Revolution, by Joyce Lain Kennedy and Thomas J. Morrow. John Wiley & Sons, Inc., 1994.

Electronic Resume Revolution, by Joyce Lain Kennedy and Thomas J. Morrow. John Wiley & Sons, Inc., 1994.

Internet Resumes: Take The Net To Your Next Job!, by Peter D. Weddle. Impact Publications, 1998.

Guerrilla Marketing Online, by Jay Conrad Levinson and Charles Rubin, Houghton Mifflin Co., 1995.

What Color Is Your Parachute?

What Color Is Your Parachute? A Practical Manual for Job-Hunters and Career Changers is the best-selling job-hunting book in the world. 20,000 people buy the book each month, and there are more than 6,000,000 copies in print. Recent reviews have called it "the job-hunter's Bible," "the Cadillac of job-search books," "the most complete career guide around," and "the gold standard of career guides." In 1995, the Library of Congress' Center for the Book listed it as one of "25 Books That Have Shaped Readers' Lives" (alongside such works as Maya Angelou's *I Know Why the Caged Bird Sings*, Saint-Exupery's *The Little Prince*, Henry Thoreau's *Walden*, Cervantes' *Don Quixote*, Tolstoy's *War and Peace*, and Mark Twain's *The Adventures of Huckleberry Finn*).

A number of common phrases in our culture: "golden parachutes," "informational interviewing," "transferable skills" etc. were all born out of this book. (The author coined the word 'parachute' to refer to career transitions, in 1968. A writer for *Life* magazine said that the odious phrase "golden parachutes" appeared for the first time a decade or more later.)

The book was first published December 1, 1970 -- self-published, in fact, by the author, using a local 'copy shop' in downtown San Francisco. The book had its first commercial edition published in November of 1972, by Ten Speed Press in Berkeley, California. It appeared on best-seller lists beginning in 1974, has been revised and updated annually since 1975; and rewritten completely in 1992, 1997, and 1998. In its lifetime, it has been on the *New York Times* Best-Seller List (paperback) a total of 288 weeks.

What do readers like about the book? In thousands of letters to the author, over the years, readers have cited the following seven things that they like about the book:

1. **The book is visually interesting to work through.** It is filled with old lithographs (some of which you will see in the body of this book), tables, charts, and cartoons. It is not just text, text, text.

2. **It works.** It gives a step-by-step process for getting around all the obstacles normally encountered in the job-hunt, which people have *successfully* used to change jobs or careers, over the past three decades.

3. **It is always up to date.** Its annual revisions allow it to keep up with the latest job-hunting techniques, and the latest changes in the job market.

4. **It is humorous.** Readers like the playfulness of the book, the cartoons and other stuff designed to make the job-hunt a little less solemn and stuffy.

5. **It has a simple, memorizable structure for doing the job-hunt or a career change, that everyone can understand:**
- **What** are the transferable skills you most enjoy using?
- **Where** do you want to use those skills? In what favorite fields of knowledge?
- **How** do you find such jobs, that use your favorite skills and favorite fields of knowledge?

6. **It takes seriously the fact that people are in a great hurry** (and thus has stuff in it for the impatient job-hunter). But it also takes seriously those who wish to be more thorough, (and thus has stuff in it for the more determined job-hunter, including a section called "Your Flower Exercises" --

a series of practical exercises for matching yourself to a job).

7. **It covers many subjects other job-hunting books don't.** Such topics as: "how to choose a career counselor," with names of counselors all over the country and the world, and "how to find your mission in life," for people of faith.

If you wish to find a copy, almost any bookstore carries the current edition. If they're sold out, or do not carry it, you can order the book (on the Web) at www.amazon.com *or by phone directly from the publisher, Ten Speed Press, in Berkeley, California, at 1-800-841-BOOK (that's -2665).*

About the Author

Richard Nelson Bolles, known the world over as the author of the best-selling job-hunting book of all time, *What Color Is Your Parachute?*, is acknowledged as "America's top career expert" (*Modern Maturity* Magazine), "the one responsible for the renaissance of the career counseling profession in the U.S. over the past decade" (*Money* Magazine), and "the most widely read and influential leader in the whole career planning field" (*U.S. Law Placement Assn.*). Dick is listed in *Who's Who In*

America, and *Who's Who In the World*, and has been featured in countless magazines (including *Reader's Digest*, *Fortune*, *Money* Magazine, and *Business Week*), newspapers, radio, and TV (CNN, Ted Koppel, on ABC's *Nightline*, Diane Sawyer, on *CBS News*, and many others).

Dick Bolles was born in Milwaukee, Wisconsin on March 19, 1927. He grew up in Teaneck, New Jersey, and graduated from high school there, in 1945. He served in the U.S. Navy, and worked as a messenger on Wall Street before attending college. The author's academic background is in engineering, physics, and Biblical studies; he is an alumnus of three institutions of higher education: the *Massachusetts Institute of Technology*, where he majored (but did not graduate) in chemical engineering; *Harvard University*, to which he transferred after his second year at M.I.T., and from which he holds a Bachelor's degree in physics (*cum laude*); and the *General (Episcopal) Theological Seminary* in New York City, from which he holds a Master's degree in New Testament studies. He is a member of Mensa and the recipient of two honorary doctorates.

He lives in the San Francisco Bay Area, is married to Carol Christen, a well-known career counselor in her own right, and has five grown children: Stephen, Mark, Gary, Sharon, and Serena (his stepdaughter). Dick's grandfather was a U.S. congressman, his father an editor for the Associated Press, and his brother was the famous investigative reporter, Don Bolles, who was assassinated in Phoenix, Arizona, in 1976. Dick's sister, Ann Johnson, lives in Florence, New Jersey.

Index

204

USENET newsgroups. *See* Newsgroups
US RESUME, 66

V

Virtual Interview, 96–97
VJF Internet Resources for Minorities, 151
Vocational tests, 83–90
Volunteering, 147–150

W

Wageweb Salary Survey Data Online, 125
Walker, Phillip A., 147
Wall Street Journal, 95, 124
Washington Post, 28, 37
Washington University, 122
Weather Channel, 118
Web and Internet salaries, 126
Weddle, Peter, 32
Weddle's Web Guide, 32, 35, 64
Westech Virtual Job Fair, 34, 65
What Can I Do with a Major in . . . ?, 122
What Color Is Your Parachute?, 194–196
Whois Lookup, 30–31
WhoWhere?, 168
Will, Gary, 57, 95–96
Williams, Eugene, 61
Women, resources for, 99, 152–154

Women's Wire, 153
WORKink, 156
World Wide Web. *See also* Internet
experiences with, 176–178, 185–187
history of, 183–185
salaries for jobs related to, 126
World Wide Web Employment Office, 22–23, 68
WWWomen, 152

X

Xiong, Rebecca (Becca), 82

Y

Yahoo!
chat rooms, 170
company directories, 132, 154
employment information, 14
list of temporary agencies, 147
professional organizations, 127
random generator, 159
small business information, 143
Yellow Pages
categories, 121
online, 128–131
Yellow Wood: Diverging Career Pathways for Humanities PhDs, 94

Z

ZipFind, 169